Water my Soul

Cultivating the Interior Life

Foreword by Eugene Peterson

Luci Shaw

REGENT COLLEGE PUBLISHING
VANCOUVER, BRITISH COLUMBIA

Water My Soul
Copyright © 1998 by Luci Shaw

First published 1998 by Zondervan Publishing House

This edition published 2003 by Regent College Publishing
5800 University Boulevard, Vancouver, BC V6T 2E4 Canada
www.regentpublishing.com

Views expressed in works published by Regent College Publishing are
those of the author and do not necessarily represent the views or
opinions of Regent College.

Interior design by Sue Koppenol

National Library of Canada Cataloguing in Publication Data

Shaw, Luci
  Water my soul : cultivating the interior life / Luci Shaw ; foreword
by Eugene Peterson.

  ISBN 1-57383-242-1 (United States)
  ISBN 1-55361-079-2 (Canada)

  1. Spiritual life—Christianity. I. Title.
BV4501.2.S465 2003   248.4   C2003-910189-4

For Eugene and Jan

CONTENTS

O thou Lord of life, send my roots rain.

G. M. HOPKINS

FOREWORD
BY EUGENE H. PETERSON

A favorite story in our home as our children were growing up was of John Muir at the top of the Douglas fir in the storm.* Whenever we were assaulted by thunder and lightning, rain sluicing out of the sky, and the five of us, parents and three children, huddled together on the porch enjoying the dangerous fireworks from our safe ringside seat, one of the kids would say, "Tell us the John Muir story, Daddy!" And I'd tell it again.

In the last half of the nineteenth century, John Muir was our most intrepid and worshipful explorer of the western extremities of our North American continent. For decades he tramped up and down through our God-created wonders from the California Sierras to the Alaskan glaciers, observing, reporting, praising, and experiencing—entering into whatever he found with childlike delight and mature reverence.

At one period during this time (the year was 1874) Muir visited a friend who had a cabin, snug in a valley of one of the tributaries of the Yuba River in the Sierra Mountains—a place from which to venture into the wilderness and then return for a comforting cup of tea.

One December day a storm moved in from the Pacific—a fierce storm that bent the junipers and pines, the madronas and fir trees as if they were so many blades

---

*Edwin Way Teale, ed. *The Wilderness World of John Muir* (Boston: Houghton Mifflin, 1954), 181–90.

of grass. It was for just such times this cabin had been built: cozy protection from the harsh elements. We easily imagine Muir and his host safe and secure in his tightly caulked cabin, a fire blazing against the cruel assault of the elements, wrapped in sheepskins, Muir meditatively rendering the wildness into his elegant prose. But our imaginations, not trained to cope with Muir, betray us. For Muir, instead of retreating to the coziness of the cabin, pulling the door tight, and throwing another stick of wood on the fire, strode *out* of the cabin into the storm, climbed a high ridge, picked a giant Douglas fir as the best perch for experiencing the kaleidoscope of color and the sound, scent and motion, scrambled his way to the top, and rode out the storm, lashed by the wind, holding on for dear life, relishing *Weather:* taking it all in—its rich sensuality, its primal energy.

⁂

Throughout its many retellings, the story of John Muir, storm-whipped at the top of the Douglas fir in the Yuba River valley, gradually took shape as a kind of icon of Christian spirituality for our family. The icon has been in place ever since as a standing rebuke against becoming a mere spectator to life, preferring creature comforts to Creator confrontations.

For spirituality has to do with life, *lived* life. For Christians, "spirituality" is derived (always and exclusively) from Spirit, God's Holy Spirit. And "spirit," in the biblical languages of Hebrew and Greek, is the word "wind," or "breeze," or "breath"—an invisibility that has visible effects.

This is the Wind/Spirit that created all the life we both see and can't see (Genesis 1:2); that created the life of Jesus (Luke 1:35 and 3:22); that created a church of worshiping men and women (Acts 2:2–4); that creates each Christian (Romans 8:11). There is no accounting for life, any life, except by means of this Wind/Spirit:

> *Thou sendest forth thy spirit [breath/wind],*
> *   they are created:*
> *and thou renewest the face of the earth.*

(PSALM 104:30 KJV)

There is clearly far more to Spirit-created living than can be detected by blood pressure and pulse rate. All the "vital signs" of botany, biology, and physiology combined hardly begin to account for life; if it doesn't also extend into matters far more complex than our circulatory and respiratory systems—namely, matters of joy and love, faith and hope, truth and beauty, meaning and value—there is simply not enough there to qualify as "life" for the common run of human beings on this planet earth. Most of us may not be able to define "spirituality" in a satisfactory way, but few of us fail to recognize its presence or absence. And to feel ourselves enhanced by its presence and diminished by its absence. Life, life, and more life— it's our deepest hunger and thirst.

But that doesn't always translate into Spirit, Spirit, and more Spirit in the conduct of our lives. Spirit, *Holy* Spirit, in Christian terminology, is God's life in our lives, God living in us and thereby making us participants in the extravagant prodigality of life, visible and invisible, that is Spirit-created.

We humans, somewhere along the way, seem to have picked up the bad habit of trying to get life on our terms, without all the bother of God, the Spirit of Life. We keep trying to be our own gods; and we keep making a sorry mess of it. Worse, the word has gotten around in recent years that "spirituality" itself might be a way of getting a more intense life without having to deal with God—spirituality as a kind of intuitive bypass around the inconvenience of repentance and sacrifice and putting ourselves at risk by following Jesus in the way of the cross, the very way Jesus plainly told was the only way to the "abundant life" that he had come to bless us with.

The generic name for this way of going about things—trying to put together a life of meaning and security out of God-sanctioned stories and routines, salted with weekends of diversion and occasional erotic interludes, without dealing firsthand, believingly and obediently, with God—is "religion." It is not, of course, a life without God, but the God who is there tends to be mostly background and resource—a Quality or Being that provides the ideas and energy that I take charge of and arrange and use as I see fit. We all of us do it, more or less.

The word "religion," following one possible etymology (not all agree on this), comes from the Latin, *religere*, "to bind up, or tie up, again." The picture that comes to my mind is of myself, having spent years "getting it all together," strolling through John Muir's Yuba River valley, enjoying the country, whistling in self-satisfaction, carrying my "life" bundled in a neat package—memories and morals, goals and diversions, prayers and devotion all sorted and tied together. And then the storm comes, fierce and sudden, a gust tears my packaged life from my arms and scatters the items every which way, all over the valley, all through the forest.

What do I then do? Do I run helter-skelter through the trees, crawl through the brush, frantically trying to recover all the pieces of my life, desperately enlisting the help of passersby and calling in the experts, searching for and retrieving and putting back together again (rebinding!) whatever I can salvage of my life, and then hiding out in the warm and secure cabin until the storm blows over? Or do I follow John Muir to the exposed ridge and the top of the Douglas fir, and open myself to the Weather, not wanting to miss a detail of this invasion of Life into my life, ready at the drop of a hat to lose my life to save it (Mark 8:35)?

For me, the life of religion (cautious and anxious, holding things together as best I can so that my life will make sense and, hopefully, please God), and the life of spirituality (a passion for life and a willingness to risk identity and security in following Jesus, no matter what) contrast in these two scenarios. There is no question regarding what I want: I want to be out in the Weather! But far more often than not I find myself crawling around on the ground, gathering up the pieces of my life and tying them together again in a secure bundle, safe from the effects of the Weather. Actually, the two ways of life can coexist; there is, after all, a place for steady and responsible routine—John Muir, after all, didn't spend all his time at the top of the Douglas fir; he spent most of his time on the valley floor. He also had a cabin that he had built with his own hands in which he received guests and prepared meals for them. But if there is no readiness to respond to the living God, who moves when and how and where he chooses, it isn't much of a life—the *livingness* soon leaks out of it.

ଶ୨୨ୡୁଡ଼

We cannot, of course, command Weather. It is there; it happens. There is no question of managing or directing it. There is no recipe for concocting "spirituality" any more than there is a chemical formula for creating "life." As Jesus most famously put it to that expert on the religious life, Nicodemus, "You know well enough how the wind blows this way and that. You hear it rustling through the trees, but you have no idea where it comes from or where it's headed next. That's the way it is with everyone 'born from above' by the wind of God, the Spirit of God" (John 3:8 THE MESSAGE).

The best we can do is to cultivate awareness, alertness, so that when the Wind blows we are *there*, ready to step into it—or not; when the absurd command comes to distribute the meager five loaves and two fish to the crowd we are ready to obey—or not; when direction is given to wait with the 120 for the promise, we are ready to wait—or not; when the invitation comes to "take . . . eat . . . drink," we are ready to come to the supper—or not.

⚬⚬⚬

The books in this series, *Growing Deeper*, are what some of my friends and I do to stay alert and aware as we wait for the Wind to blow whether in furious storm or cooling breeze or gentle breathing—intending to cultivate and maintain a receptive readiness to the Spirit who brings us Life. They are not books *about* spirituality; they are simply accounts of what we do to stay awake to the Coming. There is nothing novel in any of them; our intent is to report what Christians have commonly done to stay present to the Spirit: we pray (Wangerin), preach and teach (Miller), meditate on the soul (Shaw), reflect on our checkered experiences with God's people (Yancey), and nurture Jesus-friends (Peterson).

Our shared conviction is that most of us in this "information age" have adequate access to facts; but in regards to *Life* (*Spirit*-formed spirituality), witness and motivation are always welcome.

Eugene H. Peterson
James Houston Professor of Spiritual Theology
Regent College
Vancouver, B.C., Canada

1

GOD'S GARDEN

The Lord God planted a garden ... in Eden.

GENESIS 2:8

My Father is the gardener.

JOHN 15:1

*We need ... that wild country ... even if we never
do more than drive to its edge and look in. For it
can be ... a part of the geography of hope.*

WALLACE STEGNER

*For all that's timeless, untutored, untailored, and
untooled;
for innocence unschooled;
for unplowed prairies, primal snow and sod,
water unmuddied, wind unruled,
for these, thank God.*

LUCI SHAW

*I will ponder the glorious splendor of your majesty
and all your marvelous works.*

PSALM 145

E arly this morning, first thing, before I'd cleaned my
teeth or taken my vitamin pills, I opened the back door

and wandered barefoot in my robe across our patio and around the flower beds, pulling a wet weed here and there, nipping off dead or faded flowers so that the energy of the plant would flow into the new buds. Then over to where my tomato plants, still beaded with early dew, were standing tall against the south wall of the house. I'd planted them where the sun's warmth would reflect back on them from the house siding, doubling the heat they need to develop their luscious summer fruit. And yes, the small yellow flowers were steadily being replaced by miniature green globes of tomatoes, already looking fat enough to burst their green skins. I was convinced they had swelled and plumped out in the night! A couple of them already showed hints of a rosy blush, well on their way to ripeness. I could hardly wait for the time when I could gather them into my basket and slice them, red and juicy, into a salad or sprinkle them with sugar and salt and a dab of vinegar the way my mother used to.

I hugged myself with glee! So little work, really, for such a gratifying outcome. Now that my children are grown (and my grandchildren well on the way to adulthood) I need to involve myself with other young, growing things. I want to contribute always to new creation, to live generatively, hoping, believing that this is a part of living out the image of the Creator.

But there's a selfish aspect to it as well: the special joy of *results*, of seeing my small efforts translated into something either beautiful, delicious, or nutritious! Give the tomato seedlings rich soil, sunshine, moisture. Protect them from aphids by planting strong-smelling marigolds among them. Then watch as the growth process takes over. Such is the satisfaction of the garden for the gardener. And that gratification isn't confined just to vegetables. The velvet green of a well-tended lawn, the wisteria vines climbing on sculptured stems, the acacias with their puff balls of yellow, the vivid beds and borders of flowers and shrubs, the apple and plum blossoms, which ripen into luscious fruit, the rosy pomegranates and flame-colored persimmons, all bring their own special fulfillment to the one who has planned and tended them, in this case me, with the ready help of my husband John!

When John and I were first married in 1991 and I moved from Illinois to California, I had to learn a whole new set of gardening skills. Not only is California host to a diverse spectrum of flora quite distinct from the gardens of the Midwest and with which I was unfamiliar, the West Coast was then suffering through a seven-year drought, and many trees and plants had also been badly damaged in a freak freeze the previous December. I had to begin searching for drought-resistant *and* freeze-resistant species to flesh out the bare spaces on our property. Fortunately, there were plenty of local nurseries just bursting with enough native species to meet my challenge.

I learned to love gardening in California; it has proved to be rewarding in ways I would never have envisioned. I began to wonder: if creating a garden in an alien climate brought me such joy, how immense were the rewards God found in forming a whole new planet, complete with the Perfect Garden? And if my small, suburban garden provides me with joy and contentment as it grows in beauty and fruitfulness, I imagined how much more delighted God would be, not only with the unspoiled new world of his creation, but with me, as his creature, and with my heart responses of love and gratitude, as pleasing to him as the most brilliant flowers in any garden. Conversely, my indifference to him, my outright rebellion, my despairs and distresses would wound him even more than the brown spots in my lawn or the roses fried by a heat wave have pained me.

The First Garden, and Its Gardener

God was the First Gardener. This is not just a metaphor; right at the beginning of the world one of the first things God made was a garden. But first, God had to bring order out of chaos, as the first words of Genesis clearly imply. Any gardener who has started from scratch, wrestling with arid or rocky soil or a weed-choked square of land behind a house, will sympathize and understand that God has to be in the ordering business. Not just ordering, that is, from a seed catalog but imposing order where disorder has rampaged.

Do questions arise here for you as they do for me? Is all of creation an orderly arrangement? And how may God's creative acts show us, who are made in his image, how to be creators in our own often chaotic lives?

There is so much for all of us to observe and apply about growth and life from the kind of growth and life created and promoted by God in that first garden. It was called Eden, and every growing thing in it was designed and planted by God with purpose and faultless proportional balance and planning, climate control, a cycle of seasons, systems of nourishment and growth, of adaptation and reproduction. "The Lord God made all kinds of trees grow out of the ground—trees that were pleasing to the eye and good for food." Right from the beginning the Creator was interested in both *beauty* and *practicality*.

Though God planned this Eden garden for his first human man and woman to enjoy and profit from, the Creator himself also found enjoyment there, walking in the garden in the cool of the day, the time of re-creation and tranquillity, before nightfall. The man and woman were his groundskeepers to ensure that the garden was maintained in all its primal loveliness and fruitfulness. It must have been beautiful in the truest, most original sense of the word, full of contrasting textures, shapes, colors.

Last year, when I was moving my belongings out of my small house in Sudden Valley so that a graduate student and her family could move in as renters, I had to make multiple trips in my son's little truck up the hill from Sudden Valley and down again into the coastal town of Bellingham. I was repeatedly overwhelmed by *green* and the lushness of the overarching trees in late spring, the unfurling fiddleheads of the ferns, the upspringing ranks of grasses along the roadside—their luxuriant weediness—the rude, purposeful, unstoppable bursting of leafy-ness from rock and soil not just here but all over the globe—like multitudinous hairs growing thick from a human scalp. All those chloroplasts working away, silent, efficient, and with such radiant determination, sucking in the carbon dioxide, straining impurities out of the air, pumping oxygen back to give the animal world something to breathe! I felt I was driving through Eden. What a triumph of living color! Perhaps green was God's favorite shade in the spectrum. He certainly used a lot of it!

And I love the way God and his friends Adam and Eve could enjoy it together! I hope God enjoys walking in my heart's garden, and yours, as we welcome him there, having planned and prepared it for his enjoyment.

Eden was the perfect ecosystem, to use today's environmental term. Unblemished. Unpolluted. Thriving. And after the two disobedient human beings were banished from this garden and it was left untended, it most likely became the perfect *wild* ecosystem, a pristine wilderness.

In every sense this transition was a devastating loss both for God as well as for those two parents of the human race. Pride, self-will, self-absorption, self-deception, all sprang from the primeval source of evil that had penetrated God's perfection with its snaky head. Before Adam and Eve lay no more idyllic days of garden work and animal husbandry, no more intimate garden walks at twilight. Instead, thorns, thistles, hard labor, sweat, pain, tears. The irrevocable change had happened, and there was no going back to Eden.

God of the Wild

After the two members of God's human creation had failed him so radically, leaving the Garden of Eden in despair and frustration, looking over their shoulders at the angelic guard whose flaming sword was a vivid symbol of their being "cut off" from the perfection of their first years of life in God's unspoiled Creation, Divine Plan B went into effect. Thorns, thistles, uncontrolled weeds crowding out more desirable crops, sweat, fatigue, frustration was to be the lot of Adam and Eve, the consequence of their choice. But I have to wonder: What did God think of wildness, and wilderness? How did it fit into his purposes?

Wilderness has been defined as territory that is uncivilized, unmanaged, "nature in the raw." In Scripture, wilderness is never seen as an easy place; it is often the arena of trial and hardship, of wandering (forty years of it) for the Hebrews after they left Egypt, of solitary testing (forty days of it) for Jesus before his public ministry began. In Bible descriptions, nearly always with Middle Eastern settings, wilderness is consistently barren, dry, desolate.

But there were always special lessons to be learned in the wild, unique challenges that developed the spiritual muscles and endurance that make up the character that pleases God. By hindsight I have often found these times and places of human wilderness to be the times and places where God was at work within me, showing me where I am most dry and unproductive. But he is also showing me his resources, the things I need most—manna, springs of water, guidance by cloud (the shadowed years) and fire (the furnace of testing) along an untrodden path, challenges to action that seem beyond my human possibility but are possible with God as my leader. This was especially true during the years I mothered five children and tried to keep my own vocation as a writer alive. And even more so later, after the death of my husband, Harold, when for the first time I had to make major decisions on my own at the ripe age of fifty-nine.

I'd had a protected life with my family, at college, and with a godly husband, and suddenly I had no one to protect and guide me but God. It was, perhaps, another example of his severe mercy, to lead me into this new wilderness journey.

The Learning Journey

It is characteristic of God to call his people out into the wilderness. It's a great learning place, an unparalleled school of discipline for people like Moses and the Hebrew people, after they left Egypt and slavery behind and moved into the desert's perilous freedom; for people like John the Baptist, with his prophetic, heraldic message. There were women like Sarah, who was Abraham's partner as they left the known place of family and stability and moved into life as nomads. Or Ruth, whose journey with

Naomi was motivated by love and a search for truth. There were prophets like Elijah, who could hear God's whisper only in the solitude of exile, away from the distracting voices of his enemies. It was in the Valley of Dry Bones—a deserted wilderness if I ever heard of one—that Ezekiel saw the vision of the new life breathed by the Spirit. There were people like Jesus' disciples—his intimate men and women friends—after the Resurrection and Ascension, who walked into the untracked wilderness of living in a hostile world without his guidance and friendship. It is in the wilderness that we are forced to leave our human resources behind and where we learn total dependence.

The Parent Heart

As parents, we may wonder why God, our heavenly Parent, is willing for his children to undergo such hardships and dangers. I remember my own parental misgivings when we sent each of our sons, John and Jeff, on an Outward Bound experience before their freshman year in college. As a parent, I was indeed concerned with the possible dangers in their being dropped off by their leaders to orient themselves, and chart their own way, and solve the problems of finding food and water and shelter in the unfamiliar forest wilderness of northern Wisconsin, the possibilities of hypothermia, of accident or illness far from civilization. And their journals, when they returned, bore out all my fears! Nevertheless they both found the experience a life-changing one. They were challenged to leadership, to fortitude, to discipline, to resourcefulness, to learning how to cope with fatigue, anxiety, stress, and solitude. The risks of such an adventure were considerable. The risks were well worth the benefits.

But it is only with Jesus that this risk of the unknown spiritual or emotional wilderness is worthwhile. It's not as though we will be protected from all difficulty but that our life with Christ as companion in the wilderness will become the Great Adventure for which many of us long. Perhaps it is only when all the comfort zones provided by daily life in a complex and sophisticated society are erased that we'll be able to come face-to-face with reality—the existential truth about ourselves and our God. Risk demands faith, and faith has its eternal rewards.

Images of Health

In a world as polluted and fragmented as ours is in the twentieth century, it isn't always easy to know what health or wholeness should look like. When we are drawing an analogy between the garden and the human soul, I have found it helpful to watch for examples of health in the natural world that I can apply to soul health. Today, in settings like Northern Canada or Alaska or Siberia, or New Zealand, where I visited recently, vast forests of abundant and uncontrolled verdure and growth dominate the land.

True wilderness (when there is adequate warmth and water) is essentially a healthy and self-sustaining ecosystem from which we can learn the meaning of health, wholeness, and perhaps even holiness ("set-apart-ness").

At a deep level I have experienced the truth of this. I feel *at home* among the sparsely inhabited South Gulf Islands of British Columbia and the San Juans of Washington and in the vastness of the Inside Passage en route to Alaska. The tidal currents are swift and uncontrollable, sucking in and out through the narrow gaps between the islands; the rocks at the waterline are sculptured by wind and ocean into forms as bizarre and beautiful as the most sophisticated abstract art. Like Mole in *The Wind in the Willows* after he set off into the unknown Wild Wood and discovers that "he had never seen so far and so intimately into the inside of things," I was glad, as he was, that I "liked the country undecorated, hard, and stripped of its finery . . . down to the bare bones of it, and they were fine and strong and simple." *Fine* and *strong* and *simple* are good qualities to look for in our souls. Other adjectives that make the leap from the wilderness to the interior life could be listed, words like *noble, natural, growing, unself-conscious, unspoiled.*

But whether dry or green, strong and simple, or diverse and complex, wilderness is nature left to itself, the different elements of earth, air, water, vegetation each interacting with and affecting each other without human intervention. Perhaps God's greatest pleasure was his "unimproved" wilderness, where all the natural growth processes could continue uninterrupted and undisturbed by human intrusion. Perhaps the wilderness was less tainted by the Fall than were the human creatures in their self-absorbed pride and perversity.

Order or Chaos?

We need to draw a line between order and chaos. We need to find an equilibrium between God's ungovernable and undomesticated sovereignty—his purpose and his largesse, which is beyond our control—and our own free will, which tends to run wild and follows its own undisciplined impulses, often in destructive ways. God's overarching purposes and plans for us and our universe may seem chaotic to us with our limited perspective. But he "knows the end from the beginning." We have a prolific

God for whom extravagance is a virtue, who gives and gives, whose generosity and grace are infinite.

Driving on the highway I am often confronted by the automobile bumper sticker with the high-flown injunction: "Practice senseless acts of beauty and random acts of kindness." Appealing as it sounds, this is not quite a Christian ideal because it presupposes a meaningless, random universe without a God of grace, a bitter world that needs to be sweetened, transformed by a kind of magic wand of human goodwill. If one does not believe in God, all acts become, in a way, senseless, purposeless. All of us would agree that random kindness and beauty are to be preferred to random violence and aggression, but rather than acting senselessly and randomly, let us, in response to God's grace in our own lives, commit purposeful kindness (also known as charity) in his name and perform, deliberately, actions of unstinting compassion and generosity that will reflect God's loving nature, vibrantly alive in us.

Diminishing Creation

I've been an enthusiastic camper for years, often alone so I can think reflectively and take time to write and photograph without distraction or interruption. But my camping has always been "car camping"! If the weather turned too wet or wild I could always dismantle my tent, roll up my sleeping bag, and make my escape, snug and secure in my car. My car was my buffer, by which I could conveniently hold the wild at arm's length when it became messy or uncomfortable. In a way, it was cheating.

We diminish Creation by caricaturing it or stereotyping it or experiencing it at a remove, as do those who enter the wilderness of the national or state parks in camping trailers equipped with TVs, hot-and-cold running water, soft foam mattresses, toilets, refrigerators, and bars. And I know by experience that I can learn far more about woods and trees by watching them grow, feeling their bark, resting in their shade, than by admiring the wood grain in a polished wooden bedroom suite ordered in a furniture store, handsome though that is.

Wallace Stegner, the great California novelist, told the truth when, in a letter to his friend Wendell Berry, he said: "Wilderness is the context in which the individual makes contact with the universe." The more we distance ourselves from the elements of nature, the more abstract and unreal they become for us, the more *dis*-connected we find ourselves from them, the less we are aware of the need to protect and care for them. When our technology allows us benign access to the wilderness (as, for instance, the noninvasive raised wooden walkways that wind through New Zealand's rain forests), we grow less selfish in our appreciation of it and of our Creator. When our technology separates us from, or interrupts, natural processes, we lose our sense of their value and beauty, and once again we become dangerously self-absorbed.

Just as theology seems abstract until we gain first-hand, personal experience of God at work in our lives, Creation remains an unreal concept in the city. Where trees and grass exist only in formalized parks or where flowers grow only in window boxes, a generalized, vague idea of something appealing, but remote, is all we know of nature. A hot-house orchid has leaves and extravagantly vivid and exotic flowers, but until we see a saprophytic orchid in its tropical rain forest setting, we haven't glimpsed its essential nature.

The concreteness, the held-togetherness of creation, the real, experienced shape and contour of island and ocean closes the gap of ignorance in us, forming a bridge by which we can better apprehend the God who made us. Our idea of God, while it will always be incomplete because of our finite human nature, is greatly enhanced and fleshed out in the wilderness where we move beyond books and sermons and church buildings, which can only reveal certain selected aspects of deity.

Last summer, with eleven other intrepid souls, I joined a wilderness expedition—actually a graduate-level summer-school course with the title *Creation, Wilderness, and Technology*—among the South Gulf Islands of British Columbia. During the week we rowed an open boat for 120 miles, camping every night on a different island. Though the week chosen for the trip fell in what was usually one of the driest periods of the year, it rained most days and our clothes, sleeping bags, and the contents of our duffel bags grew steadily soggier. Unloading the boat to land for meals or to set up camp for the night, we often had to form a human chain in water up to our waists before climbing the slippery, seaweed-covered rocks to high ground, and then reverse the whole process next morning as we re-embarked. The twice-daily coastal tides were fierce, surging back and forth between the islands, and as often as not we found ourselves rowing hard against the current. Besides the practical aspects of the trip—cooking meals under primitive conditions, setting up and taking down tents—we needed to find time to read assigned texts on the environment, ecology, the theology of creation, as well as to keep a detailed personal journal and engage in discussion of the issues we recognized and faced.

Though the experience was rigorous and I often felt stretched to my limits (at sixty-seven I was the matriarch of the group), I discovered that the environment of wild and rugged beauty brought me into contact with God in a surprisingly immediate, penetrating, and life-changing way. God was calling me to a level of awareness that was new to me. It was a purgative, cleansing time. There were no comfort zones between me and the creation. I was drenched by the rain and sea water, chilled by the wind, burned by the sun (when it shone—and in a small, open ship's boat there is no escape from it), exhausted by hours of rowing against the tides (and in the process developing *incredible* upper body strength!), yet thrilled, no *exhilarated*, by the satisfaction of challenging the elements and coming out feeling heroic. I had, and have, a new respect for creation's large-ness and raw magnificence. I wrote in my journal: "I am face-to-face with the hand work of God and am left humbled and almost breathless with admiration."

The Book of Nature

Nature is God's great revelation of himself, his richness, his complexity, his intelligence, his beauty, his mystery, his great power and glory. God's fingerprints, the hints and clues to his nature, are everywhere.

John Stott has said: "God has written two books— the Book of Scripture and the Book of Nature." Next to my Bible, this is the realm where I experience God at work most powerfully. In fact, such an experience may be even more potent for me than the written Word because it is so freshly immediate. I take it in firsthand, with all my senses. I am not just reading a story about wandering in the wilderness. I have wandered there myself, feeling fatigue and hunger as well as exuberance and wonder.

It is also a joy to worship God in the riot of green and color around my house. I read Paul's ecstatic hymn at the end of Romans 11 as translated by Eugene Peterson, in *The Message:*

> *Everything comes from him;*
> *Everything happens through him;*
> *Everything ends up in him.*
> *Always glory! Always praise!*
>   *Yes. Yes. Yes.*

This has become my own song as well as Paul's. It is the credo of the *via affirmativa*, the life of celebration.

Sometimes it is only in memory that such worship is possible—when I'm in some bustling, crowded convention center or in a sterile hotel room on a business trip. That is where remembering (and journal keeping) comes to the aid of faith. Imagination is like a videotape on which the memory of green and the sounds of leaves and water are recorded. I play it again and again, and I can repeatedly recapture my sense of God's powerful presence by imaginative faith.

The Open Eye—The Gift of Awareness

Going for a walk in the woods with sharp-eyed friends is a stimulant to the soul. With my son, John, and Christa, back when she was his girlfriend rather than his wife, I entered the leafy dimness of the old-growth forest near my cabin in Bellingham, Washington. John led the way, breaking cobwebs with his face. Christa, attentive to details, bent to pick up a mottled leaf, to finger a fungus, to examine a tiny patch of lichen, or the spears of green moss which crept along a fallen tree trunk. Out of the shadows of the giant, ancient trees we emerged into the sun-drenched oasis of a small swampland, finding our way out into the swamp itself along a fallen pine tree, which formed a narrow track out across the dark, oily-looking surface of the bog. We felt as if we were walking on water! The top surface of the tree trunk had decayed into a sponge of rotting fibers from which a shoulder-high, young forest of growth had sprung—elderberries, sweet woodruff, even forget-me-nots. In the perfect silence of the leaf-skinned pond, all around us minuscule frogs hopped or dozed, drunk with sunlight. What a magic, private world we had entered, protected from civilization, but with its own predators—herons, water bugs, fish—which were a part of the ecosystem that we could not immediately observe. We stood there in the sun and mused on the fact that what we might see as chaotic has its own rules, its balances of power that we are incapable of observing or experiencing in spite of our attentiveness and close regard.

The truth is, we need more often to pay attention. And "pay" is the right word. Time and awareness, concentration and penetration are the price, the cost of seeing with both outer and inner eyes. The details are there for us to notice and appreciate. To ignore them or view them as trivial is to deny the providence of God.

When I was in New Zealand, hiking in the rain forest, I grew almost delirious with the joy of small things! My camera lens, with its zoom magnification, always helps me to consider closely what I might otherwise merely glance at and move on from: the microcosm of the moss gardens; minute, damp velvet fronds like green sea anemones and other small, low, unknown unnamed greens. Green upon green upon green, lavish, even wanton in its rich diversity of tone and texture. The brilliant, fuzzy scarlet blossoms of the rata trees. Starflowers scattered among the low grasses. My need was to stop, be still, focus, become aware, pay attention—to let speak the microcosm, the world of negligible, unnoticed things. How powerfully God can speak to us all through the ordinary, which can reach us all if we pay attention. We don't need to be world travelers, or theologians, or philosophers, or environmentalists in order to see and hear the messages of heaven in the earthly creation. "[It] is near you, it is in your mouth and in your heart" we are assured in the book of Romans (10:8). The magnifying lens of careful scrutiny brings a continual stream of unnoticed beauty into focus for the eye of faith.

My pleasure in this was so intense that it brought its own species of frustration. My passionate regret was, "So much rain forest; so little time." For God to have created a working world that functions efficiently, in which natural processes interact to reproduce and control healthy life, would have seemed, to my human understanding, completely adequate. Why the profusion of species? Why such rich diversity and complexity? Why pattern, and a spectrum of brilliant color? God must have felt the joy of an experimenter in this garden of earth, adding the grace of beauty, something nonessential in a pragmatic sense but a clear reflection of divine grace. And he places in each of us a flash of the aesthetic impulse, which needs only the smallest nudges of encouragement and expression to make us appreciate the beauty around us.

There's no monotony in God, no plodding pragmatism. If we let his richness and intricacy pervade us and inform us, how can our hearts refrain from bursting into astonished praise and worship?

We tend to think of God in terms of the infinitely huge—mountains, oceans, solar systems, galaxies, universes. But as God is beyond gender and time, so is he beyond size, glimpsed, if we open our eyes, in the helical whirl of a snail shell, the lace of veins in a leaf with sunlight behind it, or the infinite unfolding of fractal patterns as we penetrate deeper into matter and the structure of subatomic particles.

Spies for God

We Christians should be, with Annie Dillard, spies, scouts on the lookout for evidences of God at work in the universe. Our tools? Alertness, a willingness to wait and allow their reality to penetrate us, and time taken to look and to see and to record.

After that rain forest hike, I was surprised that when I mentioned moss or the uniform roundness of the gray pebbles in the stream or the striking lacy foliage of New Zealand black birches to my companions on the trip, they looked puzzled. They hadn't noticed. Deeply committed to Christian world mission, they had been discussing mission strategy. Though they were appreciative, in a general way, of the beauty of the subtropical landscape, they hadn't noticed trivialities such as moss. They weren't watching where they walked! And that seemed to me like an insult to the God who provided us with this astonishing landscape.

God of the Miniature and the Magnificent

So much for the microcosm. The macrocosm of the universe is just as fascinating, in a different way. It has an unnerving and humbling effect on us when we see ourselves as utterly insignificant in proportion to the grandeur of space with its infinities of solar systems. This is a needed corrective to our human arrogance, which in its almost unlimited self-confidence tends to view God as unnecessary, given our increasing technological advancement. Seeing ourselves *true*-ly (which means seeing ourselves the way God sees us, as finite and vulnerable, though well worth his loving attention) keeps us from the two false extremes of arrogant self-reliance and anxious insecurity.

Recently the comet Hyakutake drew the popular attention to the night skies. I was then in the hilly country of west Texas doing writers workshops with Madeleine L'Engle. One evening on our return from eating out in the small town of Leakey, we stopped the car by the side of the road, at the place we'd come to call "the star-watching place," where there were no towns, no houses, and therefore no lights in the surrounding country to dilute the sky. Deep space above us was velvet black—a wide star map. We could see the near and the far stars in three-dimensional clarity, and buzzing along below the Big Dipper was the comet, an indistinct glowing blob large enough to catch our immediate attention. We could even make out the faint path of light behind it. And though we felt awe, there was no fear in us; we sensed God's presence and power, and praised him for it.

After all,

> *What is man and woman that you bother with them;*
> *why take a second look their way?*
>   *You made them not quite as high as angels,*
>   *bright with Eden's dawn light;*
>   *Then you put them in charge*
>   *of your entire handcrafted world.*
>   HEBREWS 2:6–8, *THE MESSAGE*

Here's a question I've asked myself: Is untamed wilderness, "nature in the raw," what God had in mind at Creation, unspoiled and exquisite enough to bring profound pleasure to its Creator? Is it possible that after designing the natural world and allowing it to flourish in its feral beauty, God is saying to us, "See? This is what came of my own creative impulse. Notice how magnificent it is—this world of glory and beauty, with its aspects of health and wholeness still visible, in spite of the intrusion of sin. Now, here's your chance. I've provided you with a world of raw materials. Every garden you create holds the potential of showing you a glimpse of Paradise. Go to it, and see what kind of a garden *you* can come up with!"

2

MY GARDEN

... Making the earth say beans instead of grass.
HENRY DAVID THOREAU

Let my beloved come to his garden ...
SONG OF SOLOMON 4:16

As for recreating, if man be wearied with over-much study... there is no better place in the world to recreate himself than in a garden. There no sence but may be delighted therein.
WILLIAM COLES, 17TH CENTURY

W hen my soul is dry and thirsty and my body tense from too much desk work, airports, and boardrooms, an infallible solution is garden work.

When I garden, I don't wear a hat or gardening gloves, because I need to *feel* the sun on my head; and my fingers need to experience grit, breaking up the root balls of the seedlings as I plunge them into the watery holes I've prepared for them and tamp them firmly into place. I like the earthiness of earth, warm and organic. I like the wetness of water from the hose or watering can, and the pungent smell of tomato leaves on my hands after I've staked the plants, and the smoothness of the strap-like leaves of my agapanthus lilies as I separate and replant them. As a result, I carry dirt and green under my fingernails like a label, and though my hair is wild with too much sun and my skin is dark with tan and my back aches, God has rehydrated, *rejuiced* my spirit, and my heart sings the song of the Gardener.

Biblical Gardens

The idea, so familiar to us, of a garden for flowers where the owners can relax in privacy to enjoy their well-earned leisure seems alien to Scripture. All my life I was under the mistaken impression that the Bible was full of gardens. When I started to investigate, I found that there are really only a few pivotal ones—the Garden of Eden and the Garden of Gethsemane both come to mind. Blaise Pascal is often quoted as saying, "Man was lost, and saved, in a garden." How ironic that two places of such beauty have seen such death and sorrow, for the perfection of Eden ended in ruin and the salvation of Gethsemane was bought at a bitter price. Then there's the garden where Jesus was placed in a new tomb, near the place of crucifixion (John 19:41), and this garden saw resurrection as well as mourning.

Biblical gardens were rarely made for the pleasure of ordinary citizens. "The king's garden" (2 Kings 25:4) and the hanging gardens of Babylon, which were dubbed "pleasure gardens," were probably designed for the exclusive enjoyment of sovereigns or the very rich. By contrast, the common gardens mentioned in the Bible were essentially practical—for use rather than beauty—for growing herbs, for the cultivation of fruits or vegetables such as cucumbers and leeks, for olive groves, for orchards of fruits and nuts, for vineyards, and for grain (as in "harvest fields").

Was this practicality—the necessity of food—God's intention, once Eden was abandoned and the earth's human inhabitants were destined to eat only what they had sweated and worked for, as Genesis 3:17–18 implies? My New England mother-in-law, a prodigious gardener, always referred to the place where her superb vegetables grew in crisp rows as "the garden." For her the place of flowers was merely "the front yard." She was a very biblical woman.

In the Middle Ages, gardens were thought of as a minor replacement for a lost Eden. We grasp for such treasures instinctively, hungry for the perfection that still clutches at our hearts. Really, in much the same way that we are longing for God when we yearn for human love, what we long for in Edenic gardens is the God of Eden.

A New Beginning

Ten years ago, healing from the wound of bereavement and wanting to make a new start in a new place, I felt a distinct longing for more wilderness, more seclusion, a setting where, in J. R. R. Tolkien's words, there was "less noise, more green" than I could find in Chicago's suburbs. I decided to move west, to the foothills of the Cascade Mountains in Washington State, and build my own small dwelling place, a project on rather a smaller scale than God's. I was a widow at the age of fifty-nine, and it was my "Promised Land," the first major project I'd attempted and completed on my own in all my life. I knew I was testing myself. I was asking, "Can you cope with life alone after the death of your husband of thirty-three years? Can you embark on a time-consuming, complex project on your own and do a good job?" I needed to know if I had the capacity for that kind of responsibility, realizing that such a task, and the arduous business of relocating in the Pacific Northwest, would demand of me considerable personal growth and would probably result in increasing healing and wholeness in my life.

Why did I choose that particular plot of land? First of all, I love the Pacific Northwest, with its rain forests, its islands and inlets, its snowy mountains and deep valleys clothed in Douglas firs, Sitka spruces, cedars, balsams, pines. And Sudden Valley, where I built my house, was heavily forested and close to both the ocean and Lake Whatcom, a long, blue lake between mountains, with snow-capped Mt. Baker only an hour's drive away.

While the house was being built, I reveled in the deep seclusion of the woods around me with the sun-dappled alder trunks, luxuriant ferns, emerald mosses, vine maples scarlet in the fall, balsams busy with chickadees and their songs. No other house was in sight. A stream circled two thirds of the property, running over water-smoothed, brown pebbles, full and rushing in the winter rains, shrunken and slow but still fluid in the warm summers, and often visited by great blue herons looking for small fish. A 175-foot Sitka spruce guarded my front door. My skylights looked up at the sunlit clouds by day and the stars by night and were patterned by rain and frost in the kind of primal designs that made me feel in close touch with the Designer of the wilderness garden.

Once the house was finished and livable, I began to think about a garden. Not just a vegetable garden, though I wanted my own tomatoes and herbs. But even more elementally I wanted a kind of seamless joining between the rampant forest growth all around me and a gentler, more domesticated garden area close to the house.

At first I decided to work with what was there, making minimal changes. I hoped to capitalize on the wild bunchberries that grew prolifically beyond and below the deck, and I resolved not to move the lovely, crescent-shaped boulder that jutted out of the soil by my back door and on which I could sit outside and meditate quietly, conscious of God's presence. Instead of grass I wanted lots of ground cover that wouldn't need mowing, and I planted ivy with abandon, hoping it would grow and flourish with similar abandon. Around my "sitting boulder" I gathered and arranged other water-worn river stones and planted sweet woodruff and coral bells and Scotch and Irish mosses. I planted a little Japanese cut-leaf maple to lend its garnet color and delicate, oriental shape to the boulder arrangement. Close to the house clustered hosta, salal, columbines (both pink and white), a hydrangea, and of course a couple of the rhododendrons that grow so luxuriantly in that land of mists and rains. It was not an ambitious garden, but it suited the mood of the house, its setting, and its owner. As much as anything can be claimed as our own, I could call it mine. It looked at home in the forest setting, and having my own garden made me feel at home at last, in an indefinable sense.

The garden became, for the time being, my metaphor. Just as I had felt a close sense of identification with the creek, its rush and roar after rain, its quiet flow, cup-ful by cup-ful, almost like my stream-of-consciousness, so the garden and my plans and purposes for its growth and beauty in spring and summer symbolized the hopes I had that my own life would leave winter behind and grow free and fruitful in the sunshine of God's summer love.

In the process of planning my garden, making the most of the native plants and the available landscape, lavishing on my surroundings a lot of love and attention to detail, I became acutely aware of the joy of creating. I had moved beyond the minimal. The garden began to extend its own borders—and my workload along with it. There's an enormous satisfaction that fills your mind and body as you see a work of art take shape and become *itself*. And in that awareness God spoke to me of his own satisfaction, not only in the original, primal Creation, but in creating *me*, taking my very rough material, my weedy habits, my attitudes like stubborn boulders, my shade and sunlight, and making it into a garden for his pleasure.

Nature Isn't Neat

But for all my hopeful Sudden Valley plans I learned that nature, like the human soul, isn't neat and controlled. The local deer industriously ate the coral bells down to the ground, as well as all the new leaves off the sprouting ivy and the buds of the emerging Japanese maple. Slugs stripped the leaves of the rhododendrons and the hydrangeas. Birds pecked out the seeds I'd embedded in the soil (I was reminded of the Parable of the Sower, and the fate of the seed of God's Word, which is snatched away before it has a chance to root). I had to learn from other local gardeners what plants the deer disliked and would leave alone. I gave the slugs small saucers of beer, to inebriate themselves to death! I planted my seeds deeper, beneath the pecking capabilities of birds.

Then there were the raccoons. My raccoons were charmingly friendly, appearing at my sliding door, standing on their hind legs with their paws on the screen and engaging me in kindly and intimate conversation. Then, evidently on the strength of the friendship they'd established, they tipped over my garbage can next morning and strewed my apple peels and orange rinds the length of the gravel driveway. I learned to keep the garbage cans in the garage, protected from the furry predators.

As time went on, my sense of control diminished. Disorder increased. Moss, and later, leggy, nondescript weeds began to adorn my cedar shakes and grow in the gutters. And I learned that Sitka spruces, magnificent as they are in height and girth, are dirty trees, shedding their small cones, twigs, and resin all year round, filling my gutters, clouding my skylights. And the driveway! I'd wanted the rustic look. No urban tarmac or poured cement for me. I was satisfied that crushed gravel raked smooth had done the trick. Until the weeds began to take over. And hoeing out weeds from gravel is a never-ending, back-breaking task, as arduous as the spiritual disciplines needed to deal with the temptations on my spiritual pathway. Blackberry bushes sent out their thick, thorny stems, strong and sharp as barbed wire, to invade my garden space, threatening takeover. For me it was a powerful picture of the besetting sins that threaten to overtake our souls.

I realized that on my own level I was attempting to play God, to "tame the wilderness," that what I wanted for my garden was a level of order and control much like the kind of independence and autonomy I sometimes wish I had over my own life circumstances. In both my garden and my interior life I hoped for an environment in which untidiness and disorder had been banished—no blackberries with their thorny crowns, no fallen dead branches stranded high in the crooks of trees, no weeds, no slugs, no mildew, no poisonous spiders, no wasps to sting me, no mosquitoes to bite, no ugly, dying foliage or debris of fallen twigs and cones. Anything decaying, or untidy, or deformed, or unsightly was an offense to my senses.

Back in the sixties, when my five children were young and restless and we went to visit my elderly mother in Toronto, I was rather impatient with her dismay at all the little jelly fingerprints on her white woodwork, footprints on the vacuumed carpet, the scatter of toys and clothes. "You want to get to know your grandchildren, don't you?" I'd ask. "This is the way kids are!"

Now I'm much more sympathetic with her consternation. When two of my grown children temporarily lived with me in my Sudden Valley home, I experienced a similar reaction to *mess*, and disorder. It's the old problem of entropy. Disorder grows exponentially when the controls are lifted. I despise and abhor sterility, a naked barrenness that seems the ultimate in order and cleanliness. And I love the richness and wildness of forest and mountain passes. But not in my bed, my kitchen, my bathroom. I want to decide where I want nature untamed, and where I want orderly beauty and control. I need, again and again, to pray the words from the New Zealand Prayer Book's Order for Compline, or Night Prayer:

Lord, it is night.

The night is for stillness.
　Let us be still in God's presence.

It is night after a long day.
　What has been done has been done.
　What has not been done has not been done.
　Let it be.

The Cost of Control

Last year I attended the wedding of my son in Wallisellen, Switzerland. During the week before the ceremony we spent the best part of a day in the small, delicately beautiful surrounding forest, which even has a resident "forest manager" who cuts away the lower branches of the conifers, removes deformed tree trunks, thinning the woods systematically, trims the felled trees, each straight as a phone pole, into careful lengths, which are left in regular piles spaced along the roadside to be collected by residents for their winter fireplaces. The lacy planar growth of the pale green beech leaves (it was late April) against the dark green of the pines and firs, all neat and organized as the cut-your-own tulip fields, the close-shaven, grassy shoulders of the roads, were so tidy and domesticated that my son commented ruefully, "I think the Swiss have capitalized on neatness and organization and efficiency at the expense of joy, freedom, and spontaneity. Control is an all-important virtue for them."

Just as young parents learn, from the experience of having children, a great deal about the Parent heart of God—his delight in our growth and success, his disappointment and yearning when we ignore him or rebel against his guidelines—so the industrious and creative gardener learns much about the God who wants to make of us a garden, where with abundant water and sunshine, with heat and cold, with sowing and growing he can see the fruits of his loving labors.

It's not hard for me to draw the parallel in the growth of the soul. The reason God should take over control in our lives is to free us from our own destructive patterns and release us into joy. Yet there is a kind of Christian legalism that hopes to reign in our authentic human (and Godlike) impulses to create, to enjoy, to celebrate, to break down old, restricting barriers, to dance with God. The black-and-white mindset that draws up a list of rules, of *Dos* and *Don'ts* within which to pattern our lives, is a lot like the impulse to have everything safe and predictable and under control. It's a paranoid response to life. There's little of faith in it. It is not godlike, for God has told us, "Perfect love banishes fear" (1 John 4:18). If our lives are controlled by fear, God's love is banished instead, and we move back into the gray realm of legalism.

Unnatural Nature

I've learned by experience that a garden is a somewhat artificial concept that involves doing something with nature that nature doesn't do with itself, controlling the natural processes of plant growth in order to cultivate a space that gives human pleasure and demonstrates human control and artistry. In a garden, plants and flowers, shrubs and trees are whimsically arranged in "unnatural" groupings, with stones and grasses and ponds and walkways, all designed for the aesthetic enjoyment of the owner, who isn't likely to be happy about disorder, wildness, and weeds in the back yard.

Let me suggest again that our domestic gardens, whether for producing fruit and vegetables for food or for the beauty of flowers and decorative trees and shrubs, are one of our best opportunities to be co-creators with God, who is saying, "Over to you. Try your hand at a garden and let's see what you can make of it." Maybe what we make of it is a parable for our own soul growth, which is the theme of this book.

The Garden—An Art Form

A garden is an art form in which the gardener, the artist, gathers together and groups natural elements to produce something pleasing to the eye and meaningful to the mind. And here the word *art* once again suggests not only the artfulness of the project but the artificiality of the process. Gardens don't just happen. They have to be planned. And controlled. And cultivated.

Because they are never static. What looks neat and attractive when first planted in spring grows lanky later in the season, spreading beyond its borders, showing the ravages of plant diseases or pests, crowded by the invasion of weeds, covered with dead flower and seed heads. During the writing of this chapter I got my motivational juices flowing again by pulling up a whole border of ragged perennials that had been infiltrated by weeds and, together with John, my husband, replacing them with gaillardia, coreopsis, and multicolored daylilies. That day felt like the first day of spring for us both.

No. You can't leave a garden to look after itself.

Imagine that you have had to leave town for any of a number of good reasons and that your back garden has been abandoned for a period of weeks or months. What can you expect when you return? Will you find that the garden has continued to bloom and control itself in the way you, the gardener, have planned, or will it have reverted to weeds and "wildness"? The answer is obvious.

But another possibility is the kind of wildness planned by many gardeners today, who want to conserve their time, as they deliberately plant flowers that will seed themselves and "volunteer" season after season. This spring my sweet alyssum is coming up all by itself, white and purple, as I write this. Love-in-a-mist likewise, a happy surprise for no effort. And if self-perpetuating plants, like forget-me-nots or calendula or cosmos or bluebells or nasturtiums or lily of the valley, come up on their own, they will have stronger root systems than transplanted hothouse seedlings.

As a gardening columnist in our daily paper remarked about such self-perpetuation, "If you're on a budget, you can buy one plant, sit tight, and know that it will eventually cover an area all by itself." I'd call such self-perpetuation creative planning and aesthetic appreciation of the highest sort on God's part, a kind of insurance that beauty and grace will prevail, human effort or no.

Mint is like that. It doesn't take much to get mint going, and once it's rooted it's *there*, a permanent resident. To flavor my iced tea, to make mint jelly or mint sauce to go with my garlic-studded roast lamb, and sometimes just to refresh me by donating a leaf for me to crush and sniff as I am cultivating the impatiens. (You have to watch mint, though. It spreads underground, unseen until next year when it has taken over the whole flower bed.) Like its cousin catnip, a little bit of mint goes a long way.

Self-perpetuation is the means we've used to fill in a drab, empty area in front of our house with vinca minor. This form of periwinkle takes a while to feel at home, but once it's established it spreads beautifully. All I had to do was plug in a few plants, water, wish, and wait. God and the seasons did the rest.

My prayer is that God's work of Creation may continue in me as well as in my plants, that my soul may become his garden, whether a place of wild and spontaneous beauty like a mountainside—part of the green wilderness—or a more gentle work of God's art, in a sheltered garden with a diversity of colors and shapes, only God can determine; he loves green, and the growth it signals, in any setting. But I have faith that in my life he will see continued evidence of his loving cultivation, whether camping in the wilderness or contemplating the tranquillity of a sunny garden plot, whether watching stars or sowing seeds.

I pray that my Creator will give me "eyes to see" and a gift of attentiveness and awareness to his smallest details, which are signals of his love and care.

That if my character needs toughening he will lead me, without leaving me, through some wilderness of his choosing.

That if I am wilting or barren, unable to produce flowers or fruit, he will supply me with the kind of fertilizer that encourages growth without burning the plant.

That if I need the kind of tender, daily, loving care that I give to my houseplants, God will reassure me that I am a plant in *his* house.

That I may be able to relinquish control over my garden, yielding it into the hands of the Gardener who has my best interests at heart, who knows how to use my personal colors and growth patterns to his own glory.

3

SOIL

[In] this forest . . . an embankment with a garden of fir seedlings and ferns sprouting from it will turn out to be not soil, but a downed giant tree, its rot giving nurture to a new generation.

IVAN DOIG, IN *WINTER BROTHERS*

Earth knows no desolation. She smells regeneration in the moist breath of decay.

GEORGE MEREDITH

The best fertilizer is the presence of the Gardener.

SPANISH PROVERB

We've waited and hoped through a long, cold winter. The trees have been bare of leaves, green has been turned to brown, and then ice and snow have covered the landscape. It has been hard even to imagine what spring and summer would be like, wrapped as we have been in the iron embrace of the season of cold, death, and decay.

But after the shortest day of the year, just before Christmas, we begin to hope. We begin to watch for the sun to rise a little earlier each day and to set a little later. After the New Year, the spring seed and flower catalogs begin to arrive in the mail, full of the vivid color we've missed so much in the drab, dun-colored neutrality of

50

winter. Looking ahead, we think of Easter and hyacinths, crocuses and snowdrops, and then daffodils, tulips, and all the other resurrection possibilities of spring. Life beyond the confines of the house or heated car begins to look possible again.

And once the weather warms up we begin to get into the spirit of the thing with ever-growing enthusiasm. And the first task is to prepare the soil.

The Significance of Good Soil

First off, we may be discouraged by the quality of the soil we have to work with. Rule One is that we don't *have* to content ourselves with stony or arid soil or clay or weedy ground. Soil can always be amended. And here many hands make light work. We can order in a cubic yard of good black topsoil, transporting it in barrow loads to the flower or vegetable beds that need it most. Or we can develop our own topsoil over the seasons.

I love working along with John, my husband, to lighten and aerate the soil in our California garden, to fertilize it, digging in peat moss or the rich black compost that has been rotting behind our potting shed all winter. Onto the compost heap have gone our daily offerings of potato peelings, orange rinds, banana and onion skins, apple skins and cores, coffee grounds, wilted lettuce leaves and broccoli stalks, grass clippings—anything that will give our diligent little compost maggots and microbes something to digest and prepare on our behalf, or rather, on behalf of our garden.

Every month or so, the compost is turned, top to bottom, side to side, to aid its homogenous texture and consistency. In dry weather we sometimes have to dampen it or, in a rainy season, cover it to protect it from too much moisture. And the final product is ready when we are, dark and rich as fruitcake, organic enough to replenish our depleted soil for the new seedlings or cuttings of spring.

Trash to Treasure

I've often been amazed how time and the natural process of decay miraculously turns garbage into excellent fertilizer. Horse or chicken manure, which we might naturally regard as distasteful waste products, have a similar value when dug into soil starved for nutrients. When I was living back in Illinois I had the advantage of neighbors who kept horses and were only too glad, after they'd mucked out their stables, to contribute barrels full of their horses' fragrant "donations," which I spread over my empty vegetable plots in late fall, leaving them to leach their nutrients into the soil all winter long.

And I've been just as astonished at how our Father in heaven can transmute experiences that we can only look at with revulsion or disappointment into good use. He allows us to learn from our mistakes; just because we stumble and fall, God doesn't disqualify us from further enterprises. Though we often have to live with the consequences of our choices, those consequences are illuminating, providing us with the wisdom and experience for future decisions. On occasion, the Lord has had to let me hit rock bottom, in enough despair that life seemed to hold nothing of value for me any more. But distressing as this was, it had a clarifying effect. In the pit of desperation I could see that many of the minor issues that had so obsessed me were just that—minor. That out of the grave where I had to die to those things, God was going to resurrect me, purged clean and more prepared to face his priorities for me.

Mulling this over, I realize that God's extravagant plan for living and growing things is very different from mine. Where I might crave only life and growth and beauty, God has included the cycles of decay and death as well as thriving growth; of mold, mildew, and rot as well as healthy buds and leaves; of fall and winter as well as spring and summer. God knows that the humus from rotting trees and vegetation will make the perfect culture in which seeds and spores can germinate, and ferns, mushrooms, and spruce seedlings can grow. He planned it that way.

God of the Seasons

God, as Creator, also knows all about seasons—the cycle of earthly fertility and the spiritual seasons through which my own faith-life circles. I often tend to let my calendar fill up with speaking and writing commitments, and as a result become so overextended that I spread myself too thin, and fail to do anything with the excellence I aspire to. I am learning, though. I am actually marking into my date book weeks when nothing short of a family emergency will be allowed to intrude—weeks when I can read and sleep and pray and meditate and allow my spirit to catch up with my body. This is a real discipline, because I like to be liked, I need to be needed (I admit it, with chagrin), and I like to succeed—which is usually the consequence of diligence and intelligent effort. In this, God is teaching me the worth of humility.

The word *humility,* and *humble,* and even *human* come from the same root as *humus,* which Webster defines as "a brown or black substance resulting from the partial decay of plant and animal matter; organic part of the soil." And *homage,* the giving of honor to someone else—the servant giving homage to the master or the mistress, the conquered giving homage to the conqueror—is related to this idea of something low, basic.

When you think of it, the earth is the basis, at the bottom of all growth, at its lowest, most fundamental level. The soil is the skin of the world, above which everything else sprouts. When we talk of the "earthiness" of someone's humor or writing, we often mean that it is primitive and raw and unrefined, even coarse, much like the soil of a plowed field. Lots of things happen underneath the soil's surface—roots growing; maggots, earthworms, moles, and other subterranean creatures burrowing or tunneling—but because they're invisible, they are often ignored or unacknowledged. They are effaced because they are out of our sight.

Self-effacement, which is the human equivalent, is unappealing to most of us. We would rather be seen and rewarded for our achievements, and we more often think of ourselves in terms of success, honor, acclaimed skill, giftedness, or leadership than in terms of lowliness or meekness. Adjectives like bright, brave, aggressive, professional, prosperous are words we'd like applied to us. We want to be known as goal-oriented, innovative, entrepreneurial, movers and shakers rather than as diligent, modest, unobtrusive, or unassuming.

Pitfalls of Pride

God calls some of his people to be leaders. But the path of leadership, even when it is a divine calling, has its own set of pitfalls and temptations, as we have seen in the case of some pastors, preachers, and politicians. The most obvious is pride—the assumption that any success we have is based on our gifts, abilities, and diligence. Pride, "the last sin we get rid of, and the first to return," can become a gluttony that feeds on itself and is never satisfied.

Jealousy fits into the list too. If I've worked diligently as an assistant researcher with a prominent scientist, and the paper we cowrote for publication in *Science* is published, I'd like my work to be acknowledged. If it's not, and the head honcho takes all the credit for himself, I'll be rightly disgruntled and angry. The trick is to expect legitimate recognition without becoming arrogant. Another pitfall is independence—the false sense that we are capable of doing our jobs without help (even God's). Or power—the seductive ability to manipulate others with our incontrovertible logic or personal charisma. (And with power often comes money, even more corrosive of spiritual values.) Or "self-ism," which is today's new idolatry. While a poor self-image and a lack of self-worth may be seen as personality defects that will result in poor performance or a lack of confidence, our society has gone to the other extreme. We no longer confess, with Job, "I am a worm, and no man." Rather, there is a current over-emphasis on self-esteem without regard for what God thinks of us. Our own self-assessment has become our god.

But how can we be realistic about ourselves—learning to see ourselves truly, in perspective, rather than allowing self-ism to be our deity? Only by learning to see ourselves as God sees us. Which is even more realistic than the assessment of a child by a human parent.

It's not that God wants to dishonor us or to stomp on us or push us into the ground. But he knows that humility is basic to our soul health. It's a matter of right priority and perspective. "Pride comes before a fall." Rather than deliberately aiming to elevate ourselves, we should do the best we can with what we have and let God do the rest. "Humble *yourselves* before the Lord, and he will lift you up" (James 4:10, italics mine).

Living Metaphors

Many biblical metaphors illustrate the need for the obedience and humility of servanthood. And some of these metaphors were lived out in excruciating detail. For instance, the prophet Ezekiel who was bound with cords, "so that he could not turn from one side to another," to illustrate the bondage of the rebellious people of Judah and Israel. Jeremiah was required by Jehovah to wear an ox yoke, the heavy curves and angles of which he had to carve from wood and fasten around his own neck, like a criminal in the stocks, as a metaphor for the slavery of the people to whom he was sent as prophet. Or Hosea, who was told to deliberately marry a prostitute as a living metaphor of God's willingness to forgive and reclaim Israel. That was obedient servitude carried to an extreme that most of us would have refused or considered bizarre.

The humility of servanthood was no theoretical principle to Jesus. It was something he taught consistently through his earthly life, and hoped, perhaps sometimes ruefully, to see lived out among the twelve followers who were his most intimate friends. "If anyone wants to be first, he must be the very last, and the servant of all" (Mark 9:35). And again, "Whoever wants to become great among you must be your servant, and whoever wants to be first must be slave of all" (Mark 10:43–44).

Jesus not only taught the principle of servanthood, he modeled it, which is the most effective of teaching methods. The story told in John 13—when Jesus washed the feet of his followers, traditionally a demeaning task performed by a household slave—is not just an appealing incident that shows Jesus' intimacy with his friends. Here Jesus acted out the whole purpose of his Incarnation. He too was a living metaphor. As John Stott has written in *God's Book for God's People,*

> Jesus' actions were a deliberate parable of his mission. John seems clearly to have understood this, for he introduced the incident with these words: "Jesus, knowing ... that he had come from God and was going to God, rose from supper ..." (verses 3–4). That is, knowing these things, he dramatized them into action. Thus Jesus *rose from supper,* as he had risen from his heavenly throne. He *laid aside his garments,* as he had laid aside his glory and emptied himself of it. He then *girded himself with a towel* (the badge of servitude), as in the Incarnation he had taken the form of a servant. Next, he began *to wash the disciples' feet, and to wipe them with the towel,* as he would go to the cross to secure our cleansing from sin. After this he put his garments back on and *resumed his place,* as he would return to his heavenly glory and sit down at the Father's right hand. By these actions he was dramatizing his whole earthly career.

And that career, as Philippians 2:6–8 makes clear, involved relinquishment of his divine prerogatives and a series of humbling steps downwards. Jesus,

> *Who, being in very nature God,*
> *did not consider equality with God something to be grasped,*
> *but made himself nothing,*
> *taking the very nature of a servant,*
> *being made in human likeness.*
> *And being found in appearance as a man*
> *he humbled himself*

and became obedient to death—
even death on a cross!

Commentators have suggested that the phrase "he made himself nothing," translated in the Revised Standard Version "he emptied himself," implies the imagery of a waterfall, a flow of water continually pouring itself over the edge of the cliff, our Lord not only divested himself of his power, he poured into us the power of his love—the only kind of power that God can bless, because it is the only kind that is selfless at its root. It is that kind of giving that illustrates the spirit of servanthood and of true humility.

In 2 Corinthians 4:7, Paul describes the contrast between our inadequacy and God's power using a common household item—a terra-cotta oil lamp, the kind still common in the Middle East, oval, with a hole for the oil-soaked wick. When Paul talks about a "treasure in jars of clay" as an illustration that this all-surpassing power is from God and not from us, I believe he is referring to the flame of this oil lamp—which brings the treasure of illumination into a dark room (something that we in the West take too easily for granted), blazing out of the cracked, imperfect clay of our lives. What is seen is the light, not the lamp with all its flaws. The lesson once again taught here is the lesson of self-effacement, another name for humility.

In undisturbed nature there is a continuing cycle of breaking down and reordering as the basic elements are recycled over and over again. The rotting organic material that results from the dying of cells is reabsorbed as its nutrients are released for new spores and seeds. "Listen carefully," said Jesus, "unless a grain of wheat is buried in the ground and dies, it is never any more than a grain of wheat. But if it is buried, it sprouts and reproduces itself many times over." If even Jesus could refer to himself in such terms, how much more must we recognize that there are aspects of our human lives that need to die and be resurrected in Christ. Could that be why it is said in Scripture, "Precious in the sight of the Lord is the death of his saints"?

Cultivating the Soul's Soil

Whether a rough blade dragged by cattle or horses, as still used in many primitive cultures, or by our modern disking machines, which break up the topsoil in the field in the spring season, scooping it up and turning it upside down, the sharp, curved edge of the plow is a radical disturbance after the fallow quiescence of winter. (Have you ever, in your own garden, lifted a shovel full of loam and disclosed a colony of hysterical earthworms?) The burning off of weeds, which promotes the new growth of hay and alfalfa in the hay field, seems searing as a holocaust. John and I don't burn off the back lawn or use a plow in the home flower beds, but other tools— hoes, shovels, forks, trowels, and a small, two-cycle rototiller are at our disposal. I imagine my way into the soil, feeling the prongs of the fork or the noisy churning of the rototiller or the cutting edge of the hoe or the blast of heat from a field burn as profoundly painful and invasive, disturbing my rest or my passivity.

The prophet tells us to "break up our fallow ground." The Christian soul is all too prone to coast, rest on its oars, or go with the flow. There are a number of other expressions that imply we have lost our edge of initiative or action. "Don't let the world around you squeeze you into its own mold, but let God remold your minds from within" is how J. B. Phillips translates Romans 12:2.

In other words, we need to open our spirits to God's transformation, in an act of trust, rather than letting the pervasive and persuasive culture in which we live shape our lives and values. If we neglect our spiritual cultivation, we may have to experience the shock of God's sharp plow cutting deep into our soul's soil.

I have sometimes reflected, in a time of relative peace and tranquillity in my life, that I miss the drama of conflict and urgency, of demand and responsibility, of pain and frustration, when I am pressed into spiritual battle or when my heart is forced to cry out its desperation to God. Somehow such difficult times bring me back to the realities of good and evil, of life and death. Issues that should be in the forefront of my thinking and praying may recede into the distance unless I am jolted into new awareness.

Have you ever felt the same? Have you longed for the sharp, almost physical awareness of God's presence and the excitement of struggle against evil that sometimes comes only when you are on the front line of spiritual warfare and your own inadequacy forces you to plead for divine help? Perhaps that's why James, in his letter, reminds us that we need to "consider it pure joy . . . whenever you face trials of many kinds, because you know that the testing of your faith develops perseverance" (James 1:2–3). I like that word "develops." It has a sense of pace and personal purpose about it that speaks of God's intentionality on our behalf. He allows the struggles and trials that seem so invasive and give us such pain because he has a larger picture of reality than we do, trapped as we feel we are in our small slots of time and space. He has in mind, as most good parents have in mind for their children, an idea of how he would like us to mature, and what characteristics, and spiritual/emotional muscles we should be developing as we move in and out of struggle. And the potential that he sees in us is the reason for the various "training exercises" that he allows into our experience.

The Word, the Seed; Ourselves, the Soil

In the Sower and Soils story told by Jesus, I see myself (and I trust you see yourself) as the soil on which the seed is spread. Though this story is two thousand years old, we can, remarkably, still identify with it, finding it a vital connection with our own lives.

Notice that in the story it is not the seed that changes as the narrative unfolds but the soil. The seed, representing the Word of God, those passages or fragments of Scripture or messages from God through his creation that are able to land and take root in the soil of receptive minds, is scattered widely, it seems almost indiscriminately, by the hand of the Sower. The seed's destination, and therefore its destiny, is determined by the movement of the Sower's hand. The results, the proportion of seed that germinates, sprouts, grows high and healthy, and finally produces a crop of wheat or corn, is determined almost completely by the kind of soil on which the seed happens to be distributed. As we have seen, we can modify and improve our garden soil by adding mulch, fertilizer, compost, or other additives such as bone meal or lime.

But how do we cultivate and fertilize our souls? What spiritual "additives" will encourage our heart harvest to multiply "thirty-, sixty-, one hundredfold?" First, the cultivation, the soil preparation, which as we have already seen, may involve the plowing up of our hard topsoil, a disturbing and often painful process as the blade of the plow cuts deep.

Then comes the addition of soil conditioners and fertilizer. The spiritual and emotional counterparts of this phase of cultivation are God's introduction into our lives of his own "organic matter," anything that enriches our imaginations, our insights into Scripture, our application of the Word into life situations so that our attitudes and actions are gradually transformed. This is no quick, easy fix. The best fertilizers are not the chemical additives alone but the organic manure or compost that works slowly and deeply into the soil of our lives as they are watered by the Spirit.

We should not think only of religious practices or devotional exercises here. The enjoyment (and pursuit) of music, painting, poetry, film—the imaginative arts, the reading of literature that examines human relationships and issues through fiction and essay, the practice of reflective journal writing, the development of soul friendships with kindred spirits—all are soul enrichers provided by a loving Creator who programmed into us the need, and the supply, of beauty and meaning.

A Parable of Choice

The parables were meant to be experienced, felt emotionally rather than explained, and in fact this seed-and-soil story was one of only two for which the Lord gave an explanation to those who came to him afterwards, asking what it meant.

The gospel of Mark records that "with many parables he spoke the word to the people . . . he did not speak to them without a parable, though privately, to his own disciples, he explained everything." In Matthew's gospel, Jesus' followers asked him, "Why do you speak to the people in parables?" Jesus' answer:

> The knowledge of the secrets of the kingdom of heaven has been given to you, but not to them. . . . This is why I speak to them in parables: "Though *seeing, they do not see; though hearing, they do not hear* or under-

stand." In them is fulfilled the prophecy of Isaiah: "You will be ever hearing but never understanding; you will be ever seeing but never perceiving. For this people's heart has become calloused; they hardly hear with their ears, and *they have closed their eyes....*" But blessed are your eyes because they see, and your ears because they hear. (Matthew 13:10–16, emphasis added)

Jesus made a clear distinction between those who *want* to hear and understand, who yearn to see and believe, and those who clap their hands over their ears or shut their eyes tightly so that no shocking flash of illumination can enter. The implication here is that soul deafness or blindness is the result of personal choice. Ears and eyes that have been created to receive revelation have been allowed to atrophy—to shrivel and die—through disuse or apathy (which is itself a choice), and the result is indifference, if not active rejection, of the true Word from God. Their spiritual eyes are dulled to the brilliance of the Spirit and the colorful inner landscape of creative insight.

The parables are a hearing test and an eye test. Jesus wants both earwitnesses and eyewitnesses. Dorothy Sayers, in her treatise on creativity, *The Mind of the Maker*, suggests that we are created to see something in our minds (the imagination) and make something of what we see because we ourselves are copies ("in the image") of a Creator who saw something in *his* mind and made it. We have a high calling—to discern whether our creative insights (*in-sights!*) line up with God's special revelation in Scripture.

Good Soil

Another thing. Good soil, the kind we want in our gardens, is a mix. It's not all clay or all sand or all organic material. It's porous enough so that the pouring rain

63

doesn't pool on the surface but soaks right to the roots of its plantings.

Listen to the words of Isaiah:

> When a farmer plows for planting, does he plow continually? Does he keep on breaking up and harrowing the soil? When he has leveled the surface, does he not sow caraway and scatter cummin? Does he not plant wheat in its place, barley in its plot, and spelt in its field? His God instructs him and teaches him the right way. Caraway is not threshed with a sledge, nor is a cartwheel rolled over cummin; caraway is beaten out with a rod, and cummin with a stick. Grain must be ground to make bread; so one does not go on threshing it forever. (Isaiah 28:24–28)

Several ideas seem to be at work here. First, that God deals with us as individuals. We aren't all a silo full of anonymous "seed" to God. He takes into account the potential, the growth patterns, the variations of soil and season for which each of us is best suited. If I'm a rose, he makes sure that there's a balanced proportion of clay and sand in the soil where I'm to be planted, and once I'm in place, he digs in around my roots the bone meal that best assures plenty of buds and large fragrant blossoms.

God isn't asking me to be something I'm not. If I'm a tomato seedling he won't demand that I produce potatoes. And he's not making unpleasant comparisons as to the worth or beauty of tomatoes versus potatoes. Or magnolias versus dandelions.

In a different vein, because these verses spoken by Isaiah seem to refer to God's punishment of rebellious Israel—words like plow, break, harrow, level, scatter, thresh, beat, crush, which sound pretty violent and are traditionally interpreted as terms of judgment—we can infer that even the way God disciplines or punishes us takes our individual personalities and temperaments into account. His aim is not to destroy but to discipline, not to harm but to heal, not to fragment but to integrate, to get the best out of us, to enrich us, and to remove hindrances to our continued growth.

Feeding? Or Being Fed?

One Sunday morning I slept until 7:30 A.M., caught in a dream of frightening intensity. I was in church, before the morning service, but unprepared for my scheduled duty as a lay Eucharistic minister. Not only was I not vested, but I was in my underwear, with only a gauzy robe over it. I felt the urgent need to get home and dress appropriately and also to pick up my Bible with the Scripture passage I was to read in church.

But I couldn't find my car keys, or my car, and even the church building turned unfamiliar—a sort of Grecian ruin. Searching for the way out, I was scrambling down almost vertical stairs, conscious of my state of undress and growing panicky. Somehow I stumbled into the sacristy, but the clergy had already left. Then my rector came in, smiling, and saying, "It's okay, Luci. This is a come-as-you-are party. So, come as you are!"

I awoke with a start. I told my husband John I'd had a dream that seemed more real than the reality of waking.

I got out of bed, checked my calendar, and found that, sure enough, I was on duty for the morning Eucharist. I still felt drugged with sleep and after checking my clock I figured I could nap a little longer. When I woke the second time it was 9:35. I should have been at church by then, preparing for the 9:45 service. *The dream was coming true!*

No time to shower. I dressed hurriedly and drove the three minutes to church, realizing that I would be too late to get vested. Walking into the sanctuary I thought ruefully, "God must be teaching me a lesson about irresponsibility." I was met by our deacon who smiled and said there were already enough others serving; he didn't need me. I was flooded with relief. The Scripture lessons and the sermon were about "eating and drinking Christ." I suddenly understood: I'm here today not to serve communion but to take it, to receive the gift; not to work but to enjoy; not to feed others but to be nourished personally by Jesus; not to get vested but to come as I am, accepted because of Jesus' love for me. I realized (and the word is significant—this truth had become *real* in my heart) that vestments and ritual are externals. What matters most to God and me is the reality of being accepted, touched, and fed by Christ, and responding to that love.

For myself, and for all the ones I love, my prayer is this: *Dear God, though we may shrink from your intrusion in our lives, amend our hearts' soil, plow us, fertilize us, fill our furrows with your good seed, turn even the waste products of our lives to your use, and cultivate in us the fruitfulness we ourselves desire. For Jesus Christ our Lord's sake, Amen.*

4

SEEDS

Think of yourself as a seed patiently wintering in the earth; waiting to come up a flower in the Gardener's good time, up into the real world, the real waking.

C. S. LEWIS

Though I do not believe that a plant will spring up where no seed has been, I have great faith in a seed. Convince me that you have a seed there, and I am prepared to expect wonders.

HENRY D. THOREAU

A minor avalanche of dark, nondescript particles. They slide out of the torn corner of the printed seed packet, with its bright, colored picture, and into the narrow furrow inscribed in the soil. The seeds are unprepossessing—dry, insignificant looking—shrunken, contorted nuggets of vegetable fiber. Like other created things—animals, human beings—every kind of seed has its own unique characteristics—appearance, germination time, and most importantly its own genes and chromosomes. Though some seeds—like peas and beans and corn, pistachio nuts and pine nuts and cashews—are edible, valuable in themselves, carrot seeds are so fine they're difficult to sow in rows with any sense of evenness or control.

I can remember working in our Illinois garden when the children were small. We'd spend a whole warm spring day rototilling the soil, raking out all the old dead roots and fibers, stringy and pale against the darkness of soil (well fertilized the previous fall with horse manure). Then we'd run a taut string between stakes shoved deep into the dirt so that we could draw a straight line in its soft, rich brownness to act as a furrow, a resting place. Then—final and triumphant act—tearing the corners off the seed envelopes and sending off my small sons and daughters down the line, to bend and painstakingly drop the tiny shriveled beginnings of new life into their narrow graves. Only then were the empty seed packages slipped over the stakes at the end of the rows, reminders of *what* we had sown *where*, so that in the limbo of time between sowing and sprouting we'd have some idea of what to expect in the line of seedlings.

For it was a true act of faith. After the soil had been scattered to cover the seeds and tamped down firmly with the flat of the hoe, there was little evidence to suggest that anything transformative had happened. Invisible in their soil grave bed, we were sure, we could *feel* that the seeds were still dead, quiescent. But we hugged ourselves with satisfaction when, in the evening after the sowing, we could hear the soft splash of rain against the windows, knowing that with the night's wetness and tomorrow's warmth and light there would soon be a resurrection of sorts as those tiny seed scraps began to swell, summoning up their vital power and beginning to send sprouts *up* and roots *down*. Planting seeds inevitably changes my feelings about rain!

To look at most seeds is to receive no overwhelming sense of life or growth. They appear so insignificant (in a world that increasingly equates large size with significance), too inert, too lifeless to germinate let alone to burst into growing, leafy green plants that are capable of producing flowers, fruit, and more seeds. The whole process seems so rationally *improbable*.

Mustard Seed

Perhaps that's why Jesus, when he was talking to his friends about faith, used the unlikely analogy of "a grain of mustard," or a mustard seed—a particle of organic matter so small and dead looking it would represent a negligible fragment of human faith without apparent capacity to accomplish anything much in the kingdom of God. It seems ludicrous even to consider such small faith worth considering. But according to Jesus, even *that's* a kind of faith that God will honor and use. It's a reflection of the value Jesus placed on the small, the insignificant. Paul echoes that principle in words that encourage all of us who weren't born to honor or achievement:

> Think of what you were when you were called. Not many of you were wise by human standards; not many were influential; not many were of noble birth. But God chose the foolish things of the world to shame the wise; God chose the weak things of the world to shame the strong. He chose the lowly things of this world and the despised things—and the things that are not—to nullify the things that are. (1 Corinthians 1: 26–28)

Parables and Poems

As a poet, this idea of seeds—seminal ideas, images, phrases, the small details of human experience—is as familiar to me, in the early phases of a new poem or essay, as my own body (which has itself been "seeded," like the fertile earth, with five children, and has seen the birth and growth to maturity of these five precious human plants). I regard my imagination as the furrow, the fertile soil pocket into which the seed ideas fall, and my journal, and to a lesser degree my computer, as seed-gathering receptacles into which I can transplant the seeds once they've been recognized and have begun to grow. Like the mustard seed—something so insignificant as to be barely visible— which grows to tree height with branches sturdy enough for birds to roost or nest on, a poem or a story will in all likelihood grow from a seemingly trivial event—a passing glance, a throwaway comment, an odd phrase taken out of context, even the shape of a cow standing in a sunny field or the subtle citrus color of the rising moon—that reminds me of something else; and that something else turns out to be the hook on which a poetic line or a narrative event will hang and gather to itself other ideas and images, which eventually grow to a whole poem, a completed story. I love what Robert Frost once said: "A parable is a story which reminds us of something else, and that *something else* is always the more important of the two."

This is certainly true of the Parable of the Sower. Jesus loved those agricultural images and stories. Notice how often he called on the familiar scenes of cultivating and sowing and reaping and animal husbandry: in the Parables of the Sower and the Soils, the Weeds, the Mustard Seed, the Treasure Hidden in a Field, the Lost Sheep, the Workers in the Vineyard, the Fruitful, and the Unfruitful Fig Trees, the Sheep and the Goats, and the Growing Seed. Parables were meant to be felt. To those with no interest in the meaning, no meaning was shown. As we have already come to understand, they were emotive and evocative only to those "with eyes to see and ears

to hear," who could make the connection imaginatively—
"Yes, I see. *This* is like *that*." The Parable of the Sower is
both a seed to be sown and to germinate in receptive
minds, as well as a story *about* seeds.

Seeing the Connections

As Jesus tells this story, he makes very clear the connection between the seeds of the Word, and the soils of
our human attitudes and behaviors. This is true analogy;
each item in the story has its corresponding interpreta-
tion and application to human experience. Like most of
the other voices in the Bible—particularly those of the
psalmists and the prophets—Jesus made frequent use of
analogy and metaphor to make his point, printing its
meaning on the imagination with vivid narrative colors and
textures, which stay in the memory much more clearly and
powerfully than abstract doctrinal statements of the same
truths. Metaphor was Jesus' teaching mode of choice. I am
glad that this is so. In a way it provides a potent model
for what this book is attempting—to see in the natural
phenomena of green and growing things pictures of the
way human life works, examples in which principles are res-
cued from abstraction into living reality.

Spiritual Direction

I would also like to suggest what has been one of
the most helpful and encouraging disciplines in my own
life—that of the help of a spiritual director. There are
many terms which could be used for the person God puts
in our lives to be a companion and guide, mentor, disci-
pler, spiritual coach or trainer, counselor—all these des-
ignations give us a sense of an individual in whom we have
confidence, whose wisdom or experience surpasses our

own but with whom we sense a real kinship—a meeting of minds.

Because in our pluralistic age we have exalted the virtue of our independence, our individuality, we tend to think we can go it alone with God, helped by his Holy Spirit. This has some validity. God does see and love us one by one—as unique and special persons.

But because we are so close to our own souls, sometimes overwhelmed and buried in our struggles and stresses, it is hard for us to be our own counselors or see our problems with any degree of objectivity. Our pastors and church groups may often be a source of teaching, reinforcement, and wisdom, but often a pastor is seen as a busy authority figure, where what we really need is a reflective companion who can supply spiritual friendship on a regular, personal, face-to-face basis, and to whom we can be accountable without being slavishly dependent.

In this relationship a certain distance is essential, because an already existing friend who is our peer cannot usually give us the objective, honest counsel we need; the relationship colors both the advice and the way it is given, and we may find it hard to have our spiritual performance evaluated by a peer.

Let me tell you how I found the first individual who was my spiritual director for three years, whose help and wisdom strengthened and helped me. I had been advised by Eugene Peterson, my good friend and colleague in a writers' group to which we both belong, that as a writer who is Christian I could find immense benefit in a relationship with a spiritual mentor. Writers are people who deal with ideas, themselves powerful and even seductive. It is easy for us to fall in love with and be misguided by our own ideas, so that we need help and counsel from outside ourselves.

"But how," I asked Eugene, "am I to find this uniquely gifted person?"

"To begin with," he suggested, "pray about it, and ask the Lord to bring the person's name or face to mind. Then arrange to meet together and exchange some information about who you both are, what your spiritual journeys have entailed, and what you need in the area of spiritual direction."

I followed his advice. Since then I have had two Anglican clerics as spiritual directors. My present director is a Roman Catholic woman who is well versed in both theology and psychology, and in whose company Jesus seems especially present to me.

People and Plants

In Scripture, the way God often uses plant imagery to refer to people—human beings each brought into being as an individual, creative act of cooperation between God the Creator and the human parent—is powerfully shown in Isaiah's prophecy. He calls us "oaks of righteousness, a planting of the Lord" (Isaiah 61:3). In Illinois I lived for more than twenty years in a house surrounded by white oaks. So it's quite natural for me to be reminded of the enormous girth, height, and toughness of a mature oak tree, which springs from one of the seemingly insignificant acorns it strews around it with careless abandon, autumn after autumn. Here in Northern California, our live oaks, though quite distinctive from other varieties of oaks in their convoluted branch growth, are also constantly dropping their cone-shaped acorns, like secrets, into our flower beds, and the evidence only shows up later in the surprisingly sturdy, pale green volunteer oaklets, which, of course, we have to uproot if we choose to grow flowers rather than trees.

As a seemingly contradictory image to oaks, the same prophet, Isaiah, also suggests another metaphor—"all people are grass, their constancy is like the flower of the field. The grass withers, the flower fades when the breath of the Lord blows upon it" (a reference to human mortality?) ". . . but the word of our God will stand forever" (Isaiah 40:6–8), a reminder that both Creation and the proclamation of God's truth—the Word of God—are works that issue from God's mouth. Both represent divine purpose and priority.

But if we are puzzled by this paradox—the radical incongruity of oak trees and grass—it may help us to remember that at least a portion of our human frailty, vulnerability, and mortality, which leads to the comparison with grass and flowers, is the result of our own prideful disobedience in Eden. That's why the emphasis on weakness. It's as if God is saying, "I planned for you to be oaks—long-lived and sturdy enough to stand against the storm. Instead you chose to rely on your own strength and wisdom. See what it got you? A short, feeble life, and even during that brief life span you can't stand up to the breath, the gusts of Spirit wind that issue from my mouth." It is when we acknowledge our weakness and ask for reinforcing strength from our Maker that he is able to fulfill the promise: "My grace is sufficient for you, for my power is made perfect in weakness" (2 Corinthians 12: 9).

We see a gentler, more hopeful family picture in Psalm 128:3: "Your wife will be like a fruitful vine within your house; your [children] will be like olive shoots around your table." Once again, the agricultural images of the biblical garden—vines and olive trees—are the pictures God draws to represent wholeness and happiness.

But Dandelions?

During my college years, and until his death, my friend and mentor Clyde Kilby—a creative teacher and experimenter if I ever met one, and a great lover of flowers and gardens—made a concerted winter effort to sow dandelion seeds and cultivate the bright yellow flowers with their tooth-edged leaves in pots in the sunny windows of his enclosed porch, where he studied and entertained early-morning admirers and inquirers in his bathrobe and slippers. In a spirit of whimsical rebellion he declared that he *loved* dandelions. I think he saw in them symbols of hope and persistence. In the spring of the year he'd gather handfuls of their fluff from the airy, gray globes of dandelions gone to seed and diligently separate them and plant them in pots, hoping to encourage these blooms the color of sunlight to brighten the house during the dark, short days of the following winter. Dandelions are certainly weeds, but he thought them lovable. (As I remember, he was not conspicuously successful in his efforts to propagate them!)

After trying to rid every lawn I've lived with of these saw-toothed members of the *compositae* family, I once wrote a poem comparing a bank yellow with dandelions to the sky full of stars to which God pointed Abraham when describing the multiplicity of his coming offspring. To count them, which is impossible, is also pointless. We simply stand in awe of their potential for proliferation.

Dying, to Live

Back to seeds. It's not stretching the imagination too far to believe that Jesus likened *himself* to a seed when he said, "Unless a grain of wheat is buried in the ground, dead to the world, it is never any more than a grain of

75

wheat. But if it is buried, it sprouts and reproduces itself many times over. In the same way, anyone who holds on to life just as it is destroys that life. But if you let it go, reckless in your love, you'll have it forever, real and eternal" (John 12:24, THE MESSAGE). I respond enthusiastically to the word "reckless" used by Eugene Peterson in his translation of this verse. It has an exhilarating abandonment to it. A self-giving, risk-taking quality.

Say it again: God once dug his most precious seed, Jesus, his well-loved Son, into the arid earth of our planet and, thence, into our human hearts. From that seed, in hopeful birth, burst the green of a life lived in healing bloom and garland grace, growing into the fully formed plant that "brought forth much fruit"—a harvest of salvation. It was then that God reburied that same seed in an even darker grave bed. Glimpsing the meaning of this divine-human life, what can I ask but to have that twice rudely planted seed rooting and rising again in me so that I may be green with Christ-love, growing into his own fruitful tree?

Looking at those Scripture words again from another angle, I ask myself: What has to die in me when God plows me into the soil of sacrifice? What gift or skill of mine, given by God to enlarge his kingdom, has become so important to me that the Giver is obscured from view by the gift?

The Power of Small Things

Richard Wilbur, the great American poet, said it beautifully in his poem about a milkweed:

Anonymous as cherubs
Over the crib of God,
White seeds are floating
Out of my burst pod.

What power had I
Before I learned to yield?
Shatter me, great wind:
I shall possess the field.

The milkweed seed—*any* seed—has immense power, enough to cover a whole hillside with new, young milkweeds, enough power to fill my lawn, and my neighbor's, with dandelions.

Does this feel like a negative power? After all, how many of us yearn for the gold of dandelions in spring? But it may also be a power for good—as Jesus illustrated in his parable, the yield from one seed may be one hundredfold. Think of the multiplied power of the kernels on one cob of corn. I counted them on one such corn cob the other day—over one hundred kernels, each bursting with sweet potential. Sown and reproducing themselves—$100 \times 100 = 10,000$. By the next generation of seedtime and harvest you have a million corn kernels going to work to cover acres of prairie with green cornstalks and yellow silk tassels blowing in the wind.

I'm reminded of the power of other small things in Scripture that had large consequences—individual lives or the fate of nations changing direction. The fruit eaten in the Garden of Eden. The olive leaf glimpsed in the beak of Noah's dove. The drops of lamb's blood painted over the doorways before the first Passover. The voice that the boy Samuel heard in the night. The "still, small voice" that arrested Elijah in his wilderness despair. The bottomless vessel of oil that saved the widow and her family from starvation. For another widow, the handful of flour—all she had—that she gave to the hungry prophet. The widow's farthing. The coin found in the mouth of a fish. You can think of others. Please, think of others! Or of small events or incidents that have altered the course of your own life. Never despise the power of small things like seeds to transform the landscape of the heart.

Many seeds were created by God with remarkable mechanisms that allow them to scatter. There are the touch-me-not seeds and the pods on gorse bushes, which, when mature, explode like released springs and propel themselves far beyond the parent plant. There are seeds like those of the red cedars, which are eaten by field mice or other rodents or birds and carried far and wide to be expelled in droppings, having survived their carriers' digestive systems! In Illinois I loved to watch the downward spiraling wings, called "keys," of sycamore and maple seeds, the silk parachutes of milkweed seeds, the floating fluff of cottonwood tree seeds—all made for almost effortless dispersion by the wind, an image I find particularly appealing because it speaks to me of the power of air, breath, wind—biblical images for the powerful action of the invisible Holy Spirit: "The wind blows wherever it pleases. You hear its sound, but you cannot tell where it comes from or where it is going. So it is with everyone born of the Spirit" (John 3:8).

But the *yielding* of Richard Wilbur's poem, the *dying* and *being buried* of Jesus' Gospel words, has to happen before the harvest can be realized. That yielding, that dying, speaks of the abandonment of the self—that part of us that, weedlike, springs up to demand our own independence, our right to self-determination, our own agenda—to the will of our loving God who knows the end from the beginning and who can take the small seed of our own lives and sow it where it can grow into a bountiful harvest with eternal rewards.

5

WAITING

I wait for the Lord, my soul waits, and in his word
I put my hope.

PSALM 130:5

If we hope for what we do not yet have, we wait for
it patiently.

ROMANS 8:25

We can never be lilies in the garden unless we have
spent time as bulbs in the dark.

OSWALD CHAMBERS

Nobody sees a flower, really—it is so small—we
haven't time and to see takes time, like to have a
friend takes time.

GEORGIA O'KEEFFE

The dream of my life
Is to lie down by a slow river
And stare at the light in the trees—
To learn something by being nothing
A little while but the rich
Lens of attention.

MARY OLIVER IN *TWELVE MOONS*

*L*ike most of us in our task-oriented culture, I have often felt impatience when what I have planned or dreamed about takes too much time, doesn't immediately leap into being like a clown from a jack-in-the-box. Too often *waiting time* feels like *wasted time*.

There lies my naked front lawn. The preparation has been done. The soil has been thoroughly rototilled, fertilized with good manure or compost, raked free of old roots and debris so that it is smooth and level. The grass seed has been scattered evenly across the dark, chocolate-colored surface. Over it a layer of fine soil has been spread to protect it from the birds and from dryness under the sun's hot rays at noon. Morning and evening we remind ourselves to turn the sprinkler on, and its silver fan of drops, rising and lowering, rising and lowering, is keeping the soil moist. Everything is in place for a perfect lawn. Potentially.

But is anything happening? About a week goes by. Ten days. I begin to inspect it every day, as with a magnifying glass. Particularly if I have sown creeping bent or Maryland blue grass rather than quick-growing rye grass seed, the lag time between sowing time and growing time—visible growing, that is—seems endless. In the spring night I hear thunder and I wonder: What if we have a downpour, a cloudburst of rain, and all that precious, expensive seed is eroded away and washed across the curb and down the gutter? What if the birds have eaten the seed? What if it has started to sprout, and the heat of the sun has already killed it?

I realize I am asking some of the questions the farmer might have asked in the Parable of the Sower. It comforts me to know that the storyteller in Jesus understands my questions. Perhaps he had some of the same concerns about the Gospel seed he sowed in his friends and followers as I have about my undeveloped front lawn.

I guess—no, I *know*—I have an impatient nature. Without a good book to read, waiting for an oil change or standing in an endless line at the pharmacy or filling time when meeting a late plane is for me an exercise in frustration. I value the contemplative experience of calming down, of deep-breathing relaxation, of tarrying in God's presence, but I don't find it comes easily. Waiting often seems so open-ended, so beyond my control.

The Waiting that Enlarges

I surmise that the apostle Paul was also a restless, "type A" personality. Yet listen to how Eugene Peterson, in *The Message,* renders Paul's own words about waiting: "[Along with the creation in its birth pangs, waiting for its deliverance] waiting does not diminish us, any more than waiting diminishes a pregnant mother. *We are enlarged in the waiting.* We, of course, don't see what is enlarging us. But the longer we wait, the larger we become, and the more joyful our expectancy" (Romans 8:22–25, italics mine).

We need to realize that during the waiting times God is as vibrantly at work within us as new life and growth is at work in a pregnant mother. If through the Spirit of God we have been united with the Father in dynamic relationship, if God has sown his Gospel seed in us, then Jesus is being formed within us, little by little, day by day, just as a human embryo grows to become a fetus and develops incrementally into a human baby. But we have to wait if the Word is to become flesh, in us! And that kind of waiting feels like work!

81

If we have believed God's promise, if we have said "Yes!" to him, as Mary did at the Annunciation, we are pregnant—with God! The promise of "Christ in you, the hope of glory" is no romanticized ideal. Though not biologically visible, it is being fulfilled in us just as truly as the united genes and chromosomes of two parents may be translated into a newly conceived human being who will bear many of their characteristics.

None of us wants to be a "preemie," entering the world of harsh reality prematurely, too small, too undeveloped, and therefore unprepared to face the challenge of further growth outside the mother's body. But often it is only when the waiting is over, the baby born, that we can look back and see that those nine long months were vital to our maturity and health. "Be strong," the Scriptures encourage us, "take heart and wait for the Lord" (Psalm 27:14). Which implies that waiting requires a particular kind of strength and courage.

And of course grass seed, or any other seed, once it has the right conditions, "is enlarged in the waiting." There, under the soil, unseen but very real, a transformation is going on. The outer husk is softening, swelling, wrinkling, then splitting as the inner seed accepts the gift of warmth and moisture, and metamorphosis begins. Soon the first rootlet appears and pokes down. As it grows it splits and splits again to become a pale, lacelike thing, wrapped in its shards of grit but enormously efficient at drawing up moisture from deep in the body of the earth, where evaporation is slower. At the same time another little shoot swells and pokes up out of the split husk, piercing the dense soil above it. And when the shoot, in its upward growth, finally reaches the surface, when it first tastes air and light, its chloroplasts go to work and begin to form chlorophyll, which turns it green, along with its hairlike companions. This early growth of grass is so fine it's almost invisible. But day by day my eyes begin to notice the gradually thickening green, and I take heart. The waiting was worth it. The grass is growing! My spiritual growth may be incremental at first, hardly noticeable to anyone but God and me. But give us time. Together, in co-creativity, the new life of the believer becomes apparent, encouraged by the water of the Word, the air of prayer, the illumination of the Light of the World.

Wanting What We Want *Now!*

The lesson of waiting is of vital importance to people living in our culture—the age of instant gratification. We demand instant communication (the "snail mail" of the postal service has become too frustratingly slow and unreliable for us), and we achieve it with the clever new technologies for which our half of the twentieth century is renowned—telephones, facsimile machines, electronic mail. We want instant meals, so we pop a TV dinner into the microwave, or we whip up instant mashed potatoes. Never mind that they don't taste like much; they're *fast*!

Other created beings seem to have more of an inborn capacity to wait. I've watched bald eagles on the coast of the Olympic Peninsula, floating, waiting for the rising thermals of air, needing only to tilt an edge of feathers for a new direction or greater altitude. Even the trees in autumn seem to wait for a command (inaudible to us) that tells them, "Fall!" And then, sometimes with no perceptible breath of air, the leaves begin to fill the air with their shining flecks and line the woods with gold leaf.

In my book *God in the Dark* I tell the story of a time in Pensacola, in January, when fall finally arrives in Florida.

A pale resident of wintry Illinois at that time, I try to catch some rays on my son John's little apartment porch. Here's what I wrote in my journal:

> As I lie here in the sun . . . the wind suddenly gusts and I see a scatter of gold leaves flying down from the maple saplings a few yards away beyond the stream. I have been wanting a photographic slide to illustrate my poem ". . . let him hear," about leaves falling from the trees at God's command because they hear and obey him more instantly than we. The image in front of me is perfect. I bring camera to porch, focus, frame, and wait for the wind to blow again and release more leaves for my shutter. My skin tells me when the breeze is beginning, my ears can hear the tinkle of the wind chimes from the porch below. I take shot after shot, and only time and Kodak will tell my success or failure. But the lesson of waiting for the Spirit to move—watching, sensing the "now," obeying the breath, catching him at it—is learned, whether or not a perfect image prints itself on the film.

I remember thinking, the trees can't decide on their own to thrash around their branches. They must wait for the wind to move them. I need again and again to learn this waiting lesson from the trees. I need to tell God, "I lay my requests before you and wait in expectation" (Psalm 5:3).

Those of us who are bewildered by personal tragedies ("How can this be God's will?") or who are constantly impatient for *results* (and I include myself) need to heed the words of St. John Chrysostom, that fourth-century scholar and saint. In her book *The Cloister Walk*, Kathleen Norris quotes him as describing someone with no knowledge of agriculture "observing a farmer collecting grain and shutting it in a barn to protect it from the damp. Then he sees the same farmer take the same grain and cast it to the winds, spreading it on the ground, maybe even in the mud, without worrying any more about the dampness. Surely he will think that the farmer has ruined the grain, and reprove the farmer." Norris goes on: "The reproof comes from ignorance and impatience, Chrysostom says; only waiting until the end of the summer, he would see the farmer harvest that grain, and be astonished at how it has multiplied. So much the more, he adds . . . should 'we await the final outcome of events, remembering who it is who plows the earth of our souls.'"

Any skill that demands a long apprenticeship is bound to be unpopular. When I offer a poetry workshop students often show up wanting to be made into instant poets: "Just show me how, and I'll just do it." Inexperienced poets think the work is finished after a couple of drafts of a poem. They're shocked when I tell them I often revise my poems thirty, forty, fifty times over a period of months or years before the poem settles into itself and lets me know it's complete, the poem it was meant to be. It's not a matter of simply knowing the rules for poetry and employing them like a mathematical formula. It doesn't work that way. In *The Writing Life*, Annie Dillard tells us: "You write it all, discovering it at the end of the line of words. The line of words is a fiber optic, flexible as wire; it illumines the path just before its fragile tip. You probe with it, delicate as a worm." We listen for the line of words. We watch the image and obey it. We follow the impulse, learning as we go. The only way we learn to write is—to write and rewrite and rewrite over the years, listening to the metaphors, seeing the images, learning from ourselves and our own poems (and those of others) how language works, and trying not to shortchange either.

It's the same thing with learning to live like God, *for* God, *with* God. We won't get it right the first time. Walking, getting lost, starting over, stumbling, falling and picking ourselves up, hanging onto God's hand, listening for his instructions, learning where to place our feet, how to anticipate obstacles, allowing our muscles to toughen with exercise so that we won't fall victim to fatigue; all this training is time consuming. Maturity waits for experience to teach us. We keep hoping someone will publish a how-to book with *The Ten Easy Steps to Maximum Growth*. Wait on. And learn as you wait!

No one is enthusiastic about waiting. It's a nuisance, frustrating and uncomfortable. We wait, scowling, for better weather for the family picnic or the sail on the bay. We wait in the traffic jam, with malice in our hearts for other drivers who are slow to get their cars moving; we drum our fingers on the steering wheel, waiting for the red light to change to green. We wait in despair for a real estate sellers' market so that we can put our house up for sale. After we've sent out our college applications we wait anxiously for an invitation from the college of our choice. A father and mother wait as they watch their child's physical development, marking off the inches of height on the kitchen door, like a ladder of upward growth. At night, in a time of restless anxiety, we wait for day to break; things seem to look better in the daylight. (Listen to the refrain of the psalmist: "My soul waits for the Lord more than watchmen wait for the morning, more than watchmen wait for the morning." In that repetition we can feel the eagerness with which sunrise is anticipated by those who have to stay awake all through the long night, guarding, watching.) If we're waiting for a phone call for a date or to hear good news about a baby's birth, we grow edgy and irritable until the phone rings. "Hope deferred makes the heart sick" says one of the Proverbs.

Sailing in San Francisco Bay, sometimes John and I are becalmed, and rather than start our noisy diesel motor, we wait, because we glimpse cat's-paws of wind darkening the water on the horizon, then approaching us, closer, closer, until the sails snap full of hard air, and we adjust their trim to take full advantage of their power to propel us forward.

I'm a bread maker, and bread making, like life, takes a lot of patience. After measuring, mixing, and kneading the ingredients I must wait for the yeast to activate, to bubble up in the bread dough and raise it into a smooth, elastic, buoyant dome, so that I can punch it down again, shape the dough into loaves, and let it rise the second time before putting it in the oven to bake. And then I have to wait until it's done, brown and fragrant, before I can cool it for eating. You can't hurry baking. If you want bread that is moist and firm and fine textured you have to wait in attendance for the yeast and the oven heat to work

When we have a headache we wait impatiently for the painkiller to dissolve into our bloodstream and relieve our throbbing distress. When we've broken a leg, we wait months in a cast for that bone to heal, to knit itself into strength that will bear our weight again. And the waiting place is often the place of pain. But "let patience have her perfect work."

Seasons of Waiting

The word *Lent* means "slow." The season of Lent is a season of waiting, of watchful preparation, for the great Transformation of Resurrection. We wait not only to celebrate Christ's rising from the tomb but to experience our own resurrection and renewal as part of his body. Which gives added meaning to the long cold weeks of early spring. It all works together—the death of winter, the greening towards spring, the waking of hibernating animals and of the waiting heart.

The finale comes with the Great Vigil of Easter on that pregnant Saturday between Good Friday and Easter Sunday, a curiously blank day of further waiting in a kind of spiritual limbo. The Death has been died. It's past. The Rising is still to come, in the close future. And where are we? In the hiatus of the present. Then, in the final hours of Saturday, in the darkness of night, we begin the Great Vigil.

The word *vigil* means "an awaiting." Vigilance means watchful waiting, expectant, anticipatory. The Great Vigil is a ritual of faith and hope. Here's what happens in my Episcopal Church: We enter the church in darkness. Then a brazier full of coals is lit. Three time the words "The Light of Christ" are chanted, and as the flames leap up, the wicks of the small white candles of the vigilant worshipers' tapers are ignited, and they in turn touch other wicks into light until the whole sanctuary is pricked with small, bright, hopeful stars, which are precursors of the dawn of the Day of Resurrection. This ceremony never fails to move me, stirring my soul into gratitude that once again the cycle of life and death and new life being enacted before me has not failed, as Christ has not failed to become, once again, the world's Light. That the life of rejection and pain, and the final indignity and suffering of the Crucifixion are over.

The Paradox of Pain

After the death of my husband, Harold, I learned an important lesson about my own pain, heart pain. I learned not to dodge it, not to try to distract myself from it, not to efface it with tranquilizers or busy-ness or mind games. I had to stay with the pain, to let that deep anguish hurt, because I sensed it had a work to do in me.

Pain is an important signal; it often tells us when something is wrong, that it needs attention and therapy and time to heal. The pain of bereavement results from amputation; the "one flesh" has been cut in half. Healing from such loss is a long, drawn-out process.

Pain and Healing

Pain is also a refining fire, searching out our weak places, our most sensitive nerve endings. Because pain is so distressing, we want the pain to diminish—fast. We need thoroughness and long patience to allow our wounds to heal slowly from the bottom up without leaving infection or an abscess underneath the healthy tissue. But the longer I live, the more I realize that the place of the greatest pain is often the place of the greatest growth. Yes, pain is a part of waiting, and of growth. But "suffering produces perseverance" (Romans 5:3).

Waiting is the hardest part of the growth process. And for a seed, the waiting is done in the dark, in the black, cold, wet, airless underground. Claire Pedretti, speaking of the seed's burial in the ground, has said: "The earth grew dark and damp and cold. Shriveling hurt—until the sun drew forth from the ache a leaf."

The pain of anxiety often accompanies waiting. We begin to question if something has gone wrong. "Were those seeds outdated? Did the birds get them? What if the ground is too wet and they're rotting?" And I get anxious when a family member is late arriving for Thanksgiving or a plane is delayed. Has there been an accident? I remember one time of enormous anxiety with my husband away on a business trip while I was at home with three small children. Because of some miscommunication I wasn't sure where he was, and because of a series of events easily explained later, for three agonizing days I waited vainly to hear from him. But I'd nearly gone mad with anxiety. Fear was ruling my life. The fear was so paralyzing that in desperation I'd gone to a healing service in a nearby Pentecostal church, where a young woman prayed for me to be delivered from a "spirit of fear." The felt relief seemed a miracle. It *was* a miracle; three weeks later Harold had to travel to Israel, passing through Tel Aviv airport where earlier that month over forty people had died in a rain of sniper bullets. And I had no fear for him. I was fear free!

Answers to prayer are not always instantaneous. Time after time, as I have listened for God's voice in my life, I've heard the word *Wait! In my own good time, your prayer will be answered. You will see me at work. You will know my real presence. Your doubts will evaporate like dew when the waiting is over.* I guess the psalmist has the faith and the patience that I need when he says: "In the morning I lay my requests before you, and wait in expectation" (Psalm 5:3).

As Abraham and Sarah, and centuries later, Zechariah and Elizabeth, waited for a promised son, month after month, year after year; as Job waited for an answer to his existential questions; as Simeon waited for "the consolation of Israel," by which he meant the appearance of Christ, the Messiah; as Anna, also in those early chapters in St. Luke's gospel, waited, "with prayer and fasting" for "the redemption of Jerusalem"; as Mary waited, feeling the sword of apprehension in her heart for more than thirty years, for her son to fulfill his Father's destiny for him—they had to trust the timetable of God. They all had to wait for fulfilled promises. And so must I. And so must we all. As Welsh poet R. S. Thomas has said, "The meaning is in the waiting."

Jesus Waited

And think of all the waiting in the life of Jesus. First of all, before birth. The one who was himself the Creator, the Light of the World, the everlasting Word, yet paradoxically dumb and helpless and embryonically small, a hidden seed in the nine months' darkness of a woman's body. After his birth came the thirty slow years of apprenticeship as an obscure carpenter—the One who had crafted the universe had to wait, and painstakingly learn his human father's trade! Even after his public ministry began, Jesus told his followers again and again, "My time is not yet come." Jesus himself awaited his own sacrifice at Gethsemane with both dread and anticipation, the God in him wanting to finish the work of redemption for us, the man in him anticipating with horror the testing, the betrayal, the trial, the suffering. Even Jesus "learned obedience by the things that he suffered."

Countless saints in Scripture looked forward, including the "cloud of witnesses" listed in Hebrews 11, waiting in faith for the fulfillment of God's promises. The letter to the Hebrews tells us what faith is: "... being sure of *what we hope for* and certain of *what we do not see*" (Hebrews 11:1, italics mine).

And waiting always takes faith. Unless we hope and expect that something will happen, why bother waiting? Because the seed I have sown has the potential of germinating and covering my lawn with lush greenness, and I believe (have faith in) the instructions on the seed bag, I am willing to obey those instructions and wait for the results. As the Preacher says in Ecclesiastes: "The end of a matter is better than its beginning, and patience is better than pride" (7:8).

Waiting opens us up to possibilities we might not recognize if we leaped into action immediately. As we gain in maturity we may achieve enough objectivity to see another side to a story, or allow a shift in our priorities.

The Passion of Patience

I'm emotionally attracted to the paradoxical words *passionate patience,* a phrase coined by Eugene Peterson in his translation of Paul's letter to the Romans (5:3): "We continue to shout our praise even when we're hemmed in with troubles, because we know how troubles can develop passionate patience in us" (*The Message*). In Revelation 3 the phrase recurs, in the letter to Philadelphia, where the heavenly messenger promises: "Because you kept my Word in passionate patience, I'll keep you safe in the time of testing." As the words imply, such waiting is far from passive but reflects an attitude of watchful anticipation. Once again, in Revelation 14: "The saints stand passionately patient, keeping God's commands, staying faithful to Jesus."

Words like passionate, audacious, eager, insistent, urgent, are appropriate to describe our response to the Lover of our souls. Not tentative or negative or hesitant or full of doubt, but imperative with the confidence of faith. Yet patience, which seems to be an attempt to rein in our eagerness, is one of the nine sweet fruits of the Spirit listed in Galatians 5:22. The path to patience is a rugged one. Often we only learn it by climbing a ladder of difficulties, as Paul explains in Romans 5, with successive rungs labeled suffering, perseverance, experience, all the way up to the top rung, hope. Interestingly, the words translated *patience* and *passion* come from the same Latin root word—*pasio,* to endure. The passion of our Lord on the cross, a term often misunderstood or misinterpreted, refers to his endurance not only of physical pain but the devastating knowledge of human betrayal and rejection, added to by the cargo of our human failure, also known as sin, which burdened him, a spiritual and emotional freight adding to the load his overtaxed muscles had to carry, with his arms transfixed by Roman nails.

The apostle James instructs us (James 5:7) with words particularly appropriate for the theme of seed and growth: "Be patient then . . . until the Lord's coming. See how the farmer waits for the land to yield its valuable crop and how patient he is for the autumn and spring rains. You too, be patient and stand firm, because the Lord's coming is near." Waiting takes work. Because it is not passive, it requires determined effort. In *The Message,* Jesus says to Peter in the Garden of Gethsemane, "Can't you stick it out with me a single hour? . . . There is a part of you that is eager, ready for anything in God. But there's another part that's as lazy as an old dog sleeping by the fire" (Matthew 26: 40).

Two viewpoints:

I can see myself (and God) as the gardener, waiting for seed to sprout, for plants to grow, for flowers to bloom, for fruit to form. God doesn't ever force us into something for which we are not prepared or ready. He waits for us to grow into maturity.

Or I can imagine myself as the seed, waiting to see the Holy Spirit producing some evidence of my own soul growth in the form of leaves, flowers, fruit.

Often we have to wait for God to act. He is the initiator. We are the respondents—those who answer and obey his call to wait, to grow, to learn.

Recently I've developed a fascination for bonsai, those intentionally dwarfed trees with their miniature trunks, branches, leaves, developed so skillfully in the Far East, where patience is still a virtue. My latest acquisition is a Japanese cut-leaf maple bonsai, grown from seed, rooted in thick, green moss and river stones. Though when I purchased it, it had been growing for twelve years, it is only about eight inches tall, and correspondingly delicate; it resembles a small grove of elegant maple trees.

A bonsai is a charming example of a living art form designed and shaped to the exact requirements of the bonsai master, who waters it several times every day and takes infinite and constant care that it receives just the right amounts of sunlight and shade. He ensures this balance of outside exposure and expert protection so that it develops strongly but isn't "tested beyond its capability." Does that remind you of anything in Scripture?

The bonsai master must wait for years, clipping the tiny new shoots to the shape he desires, wiring the stems into the interesting convolutions and angles that typify oriental design, keeping the roots shallow and minimal in order to dwarf the tree in the traditional oriental style. His patient waiting is fruitful. Time is on his side, and the results justify the patience invested in the growth of a bonsai from seed to beautiful mature specimen worth hundreds of dollars.

For your soul's health, remember Luke 8:15: "Bring forth fruit with patience." Or, "By persevering, produce a crop."

Night Time—Growth Time

A friend who is a professional landscape gardener tells me that plants achieve their greatest growth at night, in the dark. True, they need the warmth and light during the day to manufacture the nutrients for growth, but the actual cell multiplication—the widening and lengthening of stems, the broadening of leaves, the swelling of buds—must occur in the darkness and stillness of night.

Night, with its darkness, speaks to us of a time when we cannot see easily. Sometimes physical seeing becomes impossible, in a blizzard, say, or in the blank blackness of midnight or when sailing the middle of a lake, surrounded by fog. It is then that we are forced to use other resources—physical, mental, spiritual—the way blind or deaf people learn to do, deprived as they may be of the easy, taken-for-granted mechanisms of vision and hearing.

Perhaps that is why some monastic orders deliberately practice sense deprivation. When the mind is no longer seduced by the sights, sounds, smells, tastes, and touches that normally surround us, it is freed to listen with an inner ear, to see with an inner eye, even to feel with inner nerves, to experience the landscape of the soul. As Annie Dillard has said in *Pilgrim at Tinker Creek*, "All I can do is try to hush the noise of useless interior babble that keeps me from seeing."

Many of my evolving ideas for themes and images in this book have come in the dark of night, when my mind is freed from the distractions or the multiple sensations that come with sight and sound and physical movement. In my nocturnal imagination I can travel widely, pulling in and focusing illustrations for the themes that add to the body of this exploration, this excursion into new spiritual territory.

I am very aware that God is a vital part of this process. Sometimes, when I go to bed and prepare for sleep, with an unresolved problem—in a relationship or regarding a conflict that I find in myself or when my creative planning hits a barrier—I can in faith drop the problem into the distillery of my unconscious mind and feel confidence that during sleep God will be putting that mind to work, sifting, brewing, refining, aging, blending together ideas and thoughts, and in the morning presenting me with solutions, or resolutions.

Faith in the Dark

Light shines in the dark but doesn't eliminate it. The "dark night of the soul" is a recognizable experience for the spiritually attuned and sensitive.

The deepest, most God-centered growth arrives with the advent of darkness, struggle, doubt. In the brilliance of noon, no faith is needed; we can see what we need to see with our eyes, no doubt about it. Faith is only needed, only invited by "that which is not seen." Have you had your attacks of agnosticism, of not being sure of anything, of feeling lost in thick darkness? I have. I'm convinced that those who have never experienced this nadir of unbelief are out of touch with reality. God's larger purposes are sometimes too large for our sin-blinded, pain-blinkered eyes to accept.

Henri Nouwen told the story of twins, waiting like seeds in the darkness of the mother's womb, uncertain of what lies ahead of them. Hearing this story I was moved to a new understanding of my present darkness, and my ultimate place in God. The twins both feel at home, where they are anxious about the journey that lies ahead of them. One of them says to the other, "Have you heard? Some day soon we'll push out into the light, and there'll be this thing called *a mother*. We'll see her face."

Now, like seeds, we are all in the darkness of the womb of God, in an embryonic phase of our eternal life. Then, emerging into timelessness, where there is no need to *wait*, in the light of the larger, infinitely more real universe, we'll see God clearly, see *his face*, which even Moses, the friend of God, never saw during his earthly life. Our irresistible urge toward growth and freedom pulls us, like the push of a fetus towards birth, into eternity, when we can see God face-to-face, where we'll know and be known. And the long wait in the dark will make the sighting even more splendid.

The seed, once buried, is essentially alone in its grave of soil. In the dark. Surrounded by the earth's deep silence. As I identify with that seed and with the waiting for germination to stir within me, the husk to split, and growth to begin, I must ask myself: What work has solitude to do in me? How can silence grow my soul? What is God's purpose in allowing me this waiting time of emptiness and inaction?

In his book of prayers, *Bread for the Journey*, Henri Nouwen tells us:

> Solitude ... is the home for our restless bodies and anxious minds. Solitude ... is essential for our spiritual lives. It is not an easy place to be, since we are ... easily distracted by whatever promises immediate satisfaction.... But if we do not run away, we will meet there also the One who says: "Do not be afraid. I am with you, and I will guide you through the valley of darkness."

In *Dakota*, Kathleen Norris reminds us that "the farmers and ranches of western North Dakota can wait years for rain.... [They whose] hopes are so closely bound with the land, speak in terms of next-year country, a region that monks tend to see as encompassing all of eternity." It is necessary for us to remind ourselves that, as the old hymn says, "Our home is in heaven, our home is not here." That the waiting time of our human life on earth, even an earth as richly diverse and captivating as ours, is a preparation for a far richer life with infinite new possibilities. "Wait on the Lord. Be of good courage. Wait, I say, on the Lord." We are, in a sense, hibernating in preparation for that eternal living.

Waiting in Solitude and Silence

Hibernation is a mysterious process. In certain latitudes the cycle of seasons comes around inevitably to winter, and as if to protect themselves, waiting it out in the safe, dark seclusion, many animals enter a different state. Their breathing and heart rates become almost imperceptible. Body temperatures drop. Metabolism slows. Sleep takes over. It is like a quiet, temporary death.

In the summer that follows, the animals—bears, other furred mammals, and fish—have been restored to full vitality, consuming quantities of food, actively foraging, hunting, mating, reproducing. What has happened in the interim?

Spring, the renewal of warmth and light, has made all the difference.

And this is so in the realms of the soul and the spirit. We, along with the rest of the created universe, await the ultimate spring of heaven and restoration of our full faculties. Like Job we can affirm: "All the days of my appointed time will I wait until my change shall come" (Job 14:14). Light will spring up and flood us with life, redeeming ("buying back") the long, dark night of waiting. "The whole creation has been groaning. . . . creation waits in eager expectation. . . . creation itself will be liberated from its bondage to decay, and brought into glorious freedom" (Romans 8:22, 19, 21).

Both my sons, John and Jeff, are cautious men. Both waited until the age of thirty-six to get married. For both of them the wait was worth it. For the marriage of John, the elder, I wrote this poem and read it during the wedding service:

Possess your soul in patience

Own it, Hold your heart the way
you'd hold a live bird—your two hands
laced to latch it in, feeling
its feathery trembling, its fledgling
warmth, its faint anxieties
of protest, its heart stutter
against the palm of one hand, a fidget
in the pull of early light.

Possess it, restless, in
the finger cage of patience. Enfold
this promise with a blue sheen
on its neck, its wings a tremor
of small feathered bones
until morning widens like
a window, and God opens
your fingers and whispers, Fly!

6

WATER

*Long before there was light, water existed, as if
chaos itself had been a kind of rainstorm.*
LINDA PASTAN, POET

*You will be like a well-watered garden, like a
spring whose waters fail not.*
ISAIAH 58:11

*Ahead ... a leaf falls from high up in a long and
gentle fall. In the water its reflection rises perfectly
to meet it.*
WENDELL BERRY

*I felt my life start up again,
like a cutting when it grows
the first pale and tentative
root hair in a glass of water.*
JANE KENYON, FROM THE POEM "HERE" IN *OTHERWISE*

At the breath of God's mouth the waters flow.
PSALM 147:18

*You visit the earth and water it abundantly; the
river of God is full of water. You drench the*

furrows and smooth out the ridges; with heavy
rain you soften the ground and bless its increase.

PSALM 65:9, 11 (NRSV)

As the rain and the snow came down from heaven,
and do not return there until they have watered
the earth, making it bring forth and sprout,
giving seed to the sower and bread to the eater, so
shall my word be that goes out from my mouth.

ISAIAH 55:10–11

Journal entry:

I am lying on a single bed in the guest house of a college in Tennessee. I have been guest-lecturing much of the day, and exhausted and spiritually drained, I have opened the window so I can breathe the fresh smell of the night as I lie under my warm bedclothes. I know that as I continue my series of daily chapel messages on spiritual renewal I need personal replenishing. I welcome the silky river of cool air as it washes across my face, reminding me of the breath of God, which can refresh my dry soul. Through the window I can actually *hear* leaves falling (appropriately enough, it is fall) with a crisp, golden sound, the way corn flakes are supposed to sound, if we believe the commercials. Beech leaves. I've been seeing them all day as I've walked around campus. They are curled and crusty enough to make an audible impact as they land on other already fallen beech leaves, ribbed in bright brown, lighter than chestnut, more like the color of a bay horse's rump and definitely not dull but varnished and glowing, a layered nation of dry leaves.

Then the click sounds of leaves falling comes more frequently, a patter with a sense of splash. This is a sound I've been longing for, a marriage of sounds. I realize it is raining.

Rain and Renewal

Rainwater and wind are both symbols of the work of the Holy Spirit in our lives, recharging our own spirits, which, in the stress of life's demands, can easily be depleted of energy and spiritual vigor.

The noise of a waterfall or the sparkling sounds of a fountain or of ripples washing against rocks in a clear northern lake or of a rushing mountain stream are all refreshing to the ear, and from the ear they penetrate the soul. The sea has the same effect on me—its endless series of breakers thundering in, sending arcs of foam lace up to my feet, then drawing back with its silver foil over the tilting sand of the shore. I think it's the fluidity of water— the way it constantly renews itself, that reminds us of the possibility, and the need, for change, and cleansing.

Though I live in dry northern California, I commute, often by car, up the coast to the state of Washington and the Province of British Columbia, where rain arrives in weather fronts that wash like waves across the northern reaches of the continent, and where day by day mist and fog gently deposit their gift of moisture, making all the gardening enthusiasts (and the gardens) happy. Driving north through the mountains of northern California and Oregon and gradually entering this aqueous zone, I feel as if my spirit is rehydrated after the dehydration of California.

When we live in one of those arid areas of our continent, what strenuous efforts we make to discover new sources of water so that once again our eyes can feast on green! In states like Arizona and Nevada and New Mexico immense sums of money and endless effort are spent developing systems that will deliver water—by canal, by underground pipes, even by low-flying planes—to maintain water-thirsty crops, parks, lawns. From our omniscient airborne viewpoint, we're all familiar with those green circles of growth that we spot in a valley otherwise completely pallid, dry, and barren. Someone has either piped water up from an aquifer or diverted it from a remote river, and the transformation of the landscape is immediate and visible. Water—the essential element for life, how can we live without it? And how can our souls survive in drought?

The Biblical Stream

Though what we would call gardens are relatively scarce in Scripture, water runs through the biblical text like a steady stream. The references to *washing* and *water* run to more than five pages in my massive *Strong's Exhaustive Concordance of the Bible*. Right at the beginning, water was an essential part of Creation: "And God said, 'Let the water teem with living creatures'" (Genesis 1:20). "And a river watering the garden went out of Eden" (2:10). And a short time later, chronologically speaking, "The waters rose and increased greatly on the earth, and the ark floated on the surface of the water" (7:18).

Yes, in the Flood, water, the bringer of life, was a tool for the destruction of a decadent civilization.

Every time I rinse my hands under the water faucet I am reminded that water was also constantly used for ritual purification according to Levitical practice, which was still in use in Jesus' time. Baptism, the symbol of cleansing, death to the old life and resurrection to the new, cannot be performed without water. Vigen Guroian, the Armenian Orthodox theologian, has said: "Water is the blood of the creation. Our bodies are eighty percent water. Water is also the element of baptism. St. Thomas Aquinas said, 'Because water is transparent, it can receive light; and so it is fitting that it should be used in baptism, inasmuch as it is the sacrament of faith.'" Even sinless Jesus, who needed no cleansing for himself, came to John the Baptizer for this ritual of water, perhaps as a model—a living metaphor of the need for human cleansing, perhaps to validate the ministry of the Baptizer (Matthew 3:13).

But though water purges and cleanses and is a potent symbol of that rigorous cleansing, it was just as often God's provision for healing and restoration. In the story of Abraham and Sarah, after Hagar, Sarah's maid, had borne Abraham's child, she was dismissed and sent off into the desert, where she and her son were destined to perish from thirst. Until. Until the miraculous happened. "Then God opened [Hagar's] eyes and she saw a well of water. So she went and filled the skin with water and gave the boy a drink" (Genesis 21:19), and that child lived and grew and became the progenitor of a nation that persists to this day.

And when Moses, leading his Hebrew nation through the desert, needed water for them to drink, the Lord provided it: "Strike the rock, and water will come out of it for the people to drink" (Exodus 17:6).

Water, the Cleansing Flow

An Old Testament promise that we often claim today is this: "Come, all you who are thirsty, come to the waters!" (Isaiah 55:1). "They will come with weeping; they will pray as I bring them back. I will lead them by streams of water on a level path" (Jeremiah 31:9). Perhaps the most familiar reference to water is the promise that occurs in Psalm 23:2 "[The Lord] makes me lie down in green pastures, he leads me beside quiet waters." And God's provision for the land is reiterated in the Psalms: "You care for the land and water it. . . . The streams of God are filled with water to provide the people with grain, for so you have ordained it. . . . You drench its furrows and level its ridges; you soften it with showers and bless its crops" (Psalm 65:9–10).

Water was a significant part of Jesus' first miracle—the changing of water into wine, a miracle that the Creator still performs wherever grapes grow, and the water that flows up through the vine allows the fruit to form and become juice and, after fermentation (another natural process from the hand of the Creator), wine.

And on and on. These pages could be filled with stories about the blessings and uses of water. Search them out for yourself, in Scripture and from your own experience!

Living in California as I have for the last six years, I have learned a great deal about water simply because the supply has been limited in times of drought. When you must restrict your daily shower to two minutes under the fierce mist of a water-saver showerhead, install toilets that use only a gallon of water for flushing, and limit your garden plantings to drought-resistant flowers and trees, your awareness of water, and its importance, is magnified. You value more whatever it is that you need and struggle to obtain or find in short supply. Try going on a long, tiring mountain hike in hot weather without your water bottle. You'll find that water, and your thirst for it, is all you can think about!

And our spiritual thirst has this almost physical aspect. We become so full of need and desire for God that our bones ache and our hearts beat faster. Listen to how the psalmist expressed his longing: "As the deer pants for water, so my heart pants for you, O Lord" (Psalm 42:1). God loves to see this thirst in us because our attention is drawn away from the thousand pursuits that leave us unsatisfied, so that our focus is directed back to himself, our only source of satisfaction, God himself.

Evelyn Underhill, in *Mysticism*, says this:

> *Meditation* is like drawing water by hand from a deep well: the slowest and most laborious of all means of irrigation. Next to this is ... *quiet*, which is a little better and easier, for ... the well has now been fitted with a windlass—that little Moorish water-wheel possessed by every Castilian farm. Hence we get more water for the energy we expend—more sense of reality.... In the third stage, *union*, we leave all voluntary activities of the mind—the gardener no longer depends on his own exertions, contact between subject and object is established, there is no more stress and strain. It is as if a little river now ran through our garden and watered it. We have but to direct the stream. In the fourth and highest stage God Himself waters our garden with rain from heaven, drop by drop.

The Oasis in the Desert

Unless we have lived in the desert, we may not be aware of the vividness of this contrast—between dryness, the result of drought, and greenness, the consequence of irrigation. It became vivid for me during a visit to Israel. One day I joined a carload of friends and drove down from Jerusalem into the arid valley through which the Jordan River flows into the salty Dead Sea. I say "down" because we dropped fourteen hundred feet as we followed the winding road from the Mount of Olives to Dead Sea level. The deeper we plunged, the higher the temperature rose until at 10:00 A.M. it had reached 115 and our skin felt dehydrated enough to crack. There, before us, in its setting of a vast, barren landscape of glare and heat, gleamed the green jewel that is Jericho.

So this is what an *oasis* means, I thought. It means hope and health where there would otherwise be only despair and death.

Just inside the town limits we stopped at a roadside fruit stall where baskets of loquats and kumquats, oranges and figs, sacks of almonds, tubs of olives, and jars of honey awaited our shekels. There was a striking contrast between the side of the street on our left that stretched, a dusty wilderness, bare and lifeless, all the way to the glittering Salt Sea, while on the Jericho side of the street grew palm trees, citrus groves, enormous, shady fig trees, and myriad luxuriant flowering vines and shrubs.

Jericho's secret? If we stood quite still and listened we could hear the gurgle of water running through the stone-lined irrigation channels, aqueducts open to the sky crisscrossing the town in every direction, pulsing with clear water rising from underground springs, making it possible for the residents to grow not only large trees but vineyards and acres of vegetables. *Water is the secret of green.* Where the aqueducts ended, the desert began again. Standing in the cool shade we could see how water had made possible the kind of garden described in Isaiah 58:11: "The Lord ... will satisfy your needs in a sunscorched land. . . . You will be like a well-watered garden, like a spring whose waters never fail."

We all need water at our roots. As the poet G. M. Hopkins cried: "O thou Lord of my life, send my roots rain!" It's the water of life, often invisibly seeping up from underground, that makes possible the visible growth—the fresh green foliage, the brilliance of colored flowers, the juicy sweetness of fruit.

Yes. This is how God responds to our human thirst and drought:

> *The poor and needy search for water,*
> *but there is none;*
> > *their tongues are parched with thirst.*
> *But I the Lord will answer them;*
> > *I, the God of Israel, will not forsake them.*
> *I will make rivers flow on barren heights,*
> > *and springs within the valleys.*
> *I will turn the desert into pools of water,*
> > *and the parched ground into springs.*
> *I will put in the desert*
> > *the cedar and the acacia, the myrtle and*
> *the olive.*
> > *I will set pines in the wasteland,*
> *the fir and the cypress together,*
> > *so that people may see and know,*
> > > *may consider and understand,*
> > *that the hand of the Lord has done this.*

ISAIAH 41:17–20

We have a God who wants to bless a multiplicity of people in a multiplicity of ways. "You're an acacia, and you're a cypress, and you're an ancient olive," he says. "You don't have to look like everyone else, and you may flourish in a different kind of environment than some of your brothers and sisters. Each of you is uniquely beautiful, but you have this in common: you all need water at your roots."

Jehovah's refreshing presence was not only offered to Old Testament peoples. It is with us today in the person of his Spirit. Isaiah 44:3–4 gives the promise, which we have already seen fulfilled: "I will pour water on the thirsty land, and streams on the dry ground; I will pour out my Spirit on your offspring, and my blessings on your descendants. They will spring up like grass in a meadow, like poplar trees by flowing streams."

We can learn a lot about the land by observing the growth it produces and the way it holds water. Driving in the countryside of New Zealand's South Island last year, from a distance we could guess the presence of a stream or even a damp seepage from a hidden spring simply by noticing the twisting line of willows that followed the water line, hugging its contours, curving between the folds and flanks of the hillsides and valleys, fitting into the niches of landscape in an invariably aesthetic way. I kept thinking, "This is such *painterly* scenery!" And we can guess something about the spiritual springs in an individual's life when greenness is evident—the verdancy of a life overflowing with the springs of the Spirit. "All my fresh springs are in thee!" is a line of poetry that resonates in us when we ourselves have tapped the source of soul water.

Water brings its own beauty with it. Desert too has its own austere loveliness, but green . . . green, what can compare with it, blessed as it is by its Creator?

And it only grows green because it's wet.

The Soul's Mirror

Water was probably the first mirror, long before glass had been manufactured, even before people gazed in fascination at their faces reflected back from highly polished brass or bronze surfaces. Of course, we see our undistorted image only in a reflection from still water. Perhaps if we had the stillness of Christ, the peace of God, deep within us we might view the world with truer perception.

How do we attain this stillness? It's a question that I need to ask myself often, pulled as I am in a thousand directions by other people's urgencies and by my own desire to accomplish things for God or, if I am honest with myself, to satisfy my own longing for significance. This afternoon I went out along the path through our front garden to our roadside mailbox to leave a letter for the mailman. I could see his truck up the road, and I was anticipating a couple of important letters, so I waited out there on the street for him to come. I was impatient, with several tasks in the house to be completed before dinner, but suddenly I was struck by the thought, "This is a chance to be still, to savor the moment." And so I waited, standing on our brick garden path, and smelled the woodsy smell of the wet, fallen oak leaves, and listened as a squirrel fidgeted noisily in the tree above me. The moss between the bricks was emerald velvet. The sky was lit with lemon-colored clouds. And I was content, glad to be quiet, and let my soul be at rest, undistracted by the slowness of the mailman's measured progress from mailbox to mailbox. For our souls' health, we need to take, or make, these moments of stillness, when we can let the world of nature, and of nature's Creator, move into our interior world and fill it with quiet fragrance and color. Refreshment. Re-freshment.

And still waters run deep, as the old proverb has it. I ask myself, would I rather be a wide, shallow, meandering river or one that is narrowly channeled between its banks, cutting deeply, over the ages, into its streambed by reason of its strong current? If I'm honest, I guess I'd like to be both wide *and* deep. Like an ocean, maybe?

Watered with Tears

Often it's our own tears that water our hearts most deeply and beneficially. Tears spring up and fill our eyes and spill down our cheeks for many causes. Though there can be tears of joy and relief—a lost child found, a marriage restored, a long wait rewarded—as in "weeping may endure for a night, but joy comes in the morning," most tears have to do with pain, sorrow, loss, grief, or remorse. Besides being a release and a relief when we are burdened or troubled beyond endurance, tears are also an evidence that our hearts are tender, touchable and teachable by God. Alan Redpath, the well-known British conference speaker, has said, "God will never plant the seed of his life upon the soil of a hard, unbroken spirit. He will only plant that seed where the conviction of his Spirit has brought brokenness, where the soil has been watered with the tears of repentance. . . ." Just as a field in early spring is moistened by the weeping of melting snow, which allows that field to be cultivated and receptive to the seed, so our souls may be watered by our tears.

And our griefs.

Grief, the Identifier

Journal entry:

A long, early walk, a circuit along Sanibel Island's Gulf Drive to the beach access and then back along the shore. The last two days a strong offshore wind has blown in, and the surf is high. I walk along the arcs of waves, avoiding the foam as it reaches for my sneakers. I note how much prettier the shells are when wet; not only does the sun catch them and gleam from them, but the color is intensified. It's easier to find and glean the bright colors where the waves are washing the

111

spread of shells because the whites are whiter and the reds, pinks, purples, oranges, are more intense. Perhaps, in the same way, crisis, trouble, grief—the breakers in our lives—show us up truly for who we are.

Because we need to know who we are.

Recently I went through deep, wrenching, private grief over a close family relationship that had become an idol in my life and needed to be relinquished. I was alone at home for the weekend, convinced that this was something I needed to work through with God alone, without calling for prayer help from friends or family. Rarely am I able to cry alone. But for three mornings I woke with my pillow damp with the tears that had seeped from me all night long, like drainage from a wound, as I felt the point of the blade in my heart. Crying out to God for his strength to do what must be done, my tears were a gift, a powerful signal to me of the reality of this deep work that God was doing in me. I felt as if God himself were crying *with* me. Like the psalmist who asked God to put his tears in his bottle, I knew those rare drops were precious. And after the three days of mourning I felt flooded with peace. My soul had been watered; like spring rain, tears had turned my soil soft and malleable enough for God to enter and make things right between us. Tears let me know that he was with me in the letting go and in the resurrection of new growth in my soul. Like the psalmist, I was grateful that "My tears have been my food, day and night" (Psalm 42:3).

I often feel the cultivating tools of God at work on the surface of my soul, so brightly hard and shiny, but underneath so dry and thirsty. The hoe chips away at me. Sometimes, when these painful invasions of God's cultivation convict me of wrongdoing or a resentful, unforgiving attitude or exaggeration to the point of falsehood, my tears will start coming in penitence, cleansing, and also in the watering of my interior soil. My tears, like rain, are an apt symbol. As long as I can weep, as long as tears can well up and brim over from my eyes, I know that I am not completely dried out!

And *non sine sole iris*, "no rainbow without the sun." No rainbow without the rain either.

A muddy corm
(encouraged by
a south wall and a warm
wet, silver shower)
will glow, topaz
in a crocus flower.

Let April show
more wonder—
out of those soft, dull clouds
lightning spears thunder,
living storm
dissolves gray shrouds
of snow,
brown blankets of shaggy sod
turn emerald.
Why doubt?
The sullen reprobate,
the sodden clod,
the heart of hate,
the darkened face,
the old,
watered and warmed by grace
may sprout
and grow up green and gold
for God.

7

GROWING IN THE LIGHT

Who would have thought my shrivel'd heart
Could have recovered greennesse? It was gone
Quite underground.

GEORGE HERBERT

This land that was laid waste has become like the
garden of Eden.

EZEKIEL 36:35

The air is filled with south ...
Breath which though soft, unseen,
Pants warm from some far tropic mouth
And mists the world with Green.

LUCI SHAW

Faith is not a leap into the dark, but into the light.

JOHN POLKINGHORNE

*A*nd now we arrive at the underlying reason for this book, the goal of all the preparation that has gone before. The growth of the seed, and the soul, into green vitality and burgeoning splendor.

The seed has germinated and is pushing up. Think, for a moment, of its single-mindedness! All its juicy energy is channeled into launching itself up through the loam to the light, which draws it like a magnet. We have all heard the stories of concrete pavements cracked and split apart by the almost unbelievable, irresistible force of a tender green plant, which in all its fragility (it could be so easily crushed under my heel) has conquered concrete. Scientists can tell us, astonishing us, how many pounds of pressure per square inch such a plant achieves. Its force is indomitable. It will not be kept down.

I was transfixed, once, during a dinner party I was hosting for friends, by the sudden sight, in my own dining room, of a green vine spiraling up artistically out of the spout of a blue-and-white teapot as it sat next to the wall on my credenza. It had a surprised look as if to query, "What am I doing here?" Closer investigation (after the guests had departed) revealed its source as a dried pea hidden inside the teapot. My conjecture was that in some time in the dim past, one of my young sons had been prodigal with his peashooter in the dining room, and the vagrant pea, nurtured at last by moisture of unknown origin, had been encouraged enough to sprout and wind its way in the dark towards the tiny star of light that shone through the teapot spout.

And the young plant shrouded in the soil "knows," senses, that its task is to reach the light. That it is destined for resurrection after its long burial—that to arrive in the light will mean life and health and fruitfulness. Even the down-branching roots are part of this vegetable flourishing in one upward direction; as the rootlets anchor the shoot, they send the sucked-in moisture and fresh nutrients back up to the sprout's growing edges, its rudimentary leaves. And when those tiny leaves thicken and spread and turn green, they too become miniature food factories

115

for the plant, and the new growth continues to shoot up like the stories added to a house under construction.

Light and Darkness

Light, one of the most basic necessities for plant and animal life, is so assumed by most of us to be a part of our status quo that we rarely reflect on it unless we are scientists or philosophers. Yet light without darkness is meaningless. Darkness without light is absurdity. A light source always creates shadows. A dark room shows up every pinpoint of light for what it is. God gives us darkness so that we can experience the presence or absence of light, and appreciate the difference. Contrast is vital to the perception of value.

A technique among painters of the Italian Renaissance was known as *chiaroscuro*, literally "clear/obscure," or "light/shadow." In this artistic style the facial features and prominent folds of cloth or metallic ornaments in a portrait were dramatized by being painted in golden or pale tones while the other features were sunk in shadow with more somber pigments. The contrast, even today, is startling and gives an illusion of depth.

Light speaks of truth, of lucidity, of enlightenment, of revelation. I am reminded of the puzzling words in John 21:12, following Jesus' resurrection, "Now none of the disciples dared to ask him 'Who are you?' because they knew it was the Lord." Here was the classic split between cognition and recognition. Their eyes convinced them of Jesus' identity at the rational, physical level. But emotionally and spiritually they were unsure, unready for the risk of faith that would proclaim their certainty that he was the one who had been the Master of their lives for the last three and a half years.

In Philippians 3:14 the NIV retranslates the King James' phrase "the high calling" as "the upward pull" of God in Christ Jesus. This makes clear the dual nature of reality that is both material and spiritual, visible and invisible, temporal and eternal. God, like the sun with its gravitational pull that draws the new seedling up from its dark earth sheath into light and air, is calling us upward to himself, away from our blind preoccupation with a world that can satisfy only a part of us, as we apprehend it with our senses. God himself, if we are in a faith relationship with him, is the new realm in which we live and move and have our being. His immanence fills all the cracks in our materiality. I love the Bible verse that proclaims, "The earth will be full of the knowledge of the Lord as the waters cover the sea" (Isaiah 11:9).

We can no more grow and bear flowers and fruit while existing in the dark than a garden can grow and flourish underground. We need the diurnal rhythms of night and day, light and darkness. The night makes us appreciate daybreak. Our periods of spiritual shadow—the "dark night of the soul" when doubt seems to overwhelm us and God seems to have gone away (and was he ever really with us?)—make the epiphany all the more welcome.

The Single-minded Soul

All this brings vividly to my consciousness the single-mindedness that God honors in his human children. Again and again in Scripture the theme of wholehearted desire for God appears and reappears in words like this, spoken by Paul the Apostle: "[This] one thing I do: Forgetting what is behind and straining toward what is ahead, I press on toward the goal to win the prize for which God has called me heavenward in Christ Jesus" (Philippians

3:13–14). Jesus' words "If your eye is single, your whole body will be full of light" tell the simplicity of single-mindedness, of clear-eyed upward focus on the God who loves us, which has been the desire of Christian mystics like Julian of Norwich and Clare of Assisi and Thérèse of Lisieux and John of the Cross.

Another verse, this time from a singer-poet, "As the deer pants for streams of water, so my soul pants for you, O God" (Psalm 42:1). I love what Dietrich Bonhoeffer said about these verses: "Have you ever, on a cold autumn night in the forest, heard the piercing cry of a deer? The whole forest shudders with the cry of longing. In the same way . . . a human soul longs, not for some earthly good, but for God (in *Testament to Freedom*).

This kind of powerful imagery, so often used in the psalms to describe human emotion, compares the desperation of physical thirst to the deep heart thirst for God, the only one who can satisfy that thirst. "O God, . . . earnestly I seek you; my soul thirsts for you, my body longs for you, in a dry and weary land where there is no water" (Psalm 63:1). Or this: "One thing I ask of the Lord, this is what I seek: that I may dwell in the house of the Lord all the days of my life, to gaze upon the beauty of the Lord, and to seek him in his temple" (Psalm 27:4). One thing? Was being in God's beautiful presence truly the sole desire of the psalmist? Was he speaking with hyperbole? Was he overstating his devotion to God to make an emphatic point or set an example?

I fervently want to follow the psalmist's example, if he was speaking literally. But too often I find myself fragmented; I am continually asking God for *things* (in the plural), "All these things I ask of the Lord"—many, many things, helpful, entirely appropriate things I keep reassuring myself—untroubled sleep for a tired husband, rain for my dry garden, spiritual health for my children and my church, comfort for a bereaved friend, growth in grace, clarity and creativity in my thinking as I write. Our petitionary prayer lists are long and urgent.

But is there one thing that, if I attained it, would capture and include all these other graces and blessings? Jesus certainly seemed to think so. Remember the rich, young ruler of Mark 10:17–22? He was a seeker, a successful executive who came to Jesus with one of those existential questions: "What must I do to inherit eternal life?" Jesus reminded him of the usual answers that prevailed, and still prevail, in the religious community: "Do not murder, do not commit adultery, do not steal, do not give false testimony, do not defraud, honor your father and your mother . . ." As the young man checked off these items on the list with (we guess) an air of confident complacency, Jesus must have looked him in the eye, loving the expectant heart desire that lay behind all this exemplary behavior, and putting his finger on the one trouble spot in the young man's life—his materialism, his love of possessions, "for he had great wealth." That was the one thing he couldn't bring himself to relinquish. And he went away sad and unfulfilled because his life was so bound up in temporal wealth that he was blinded to the treasure he could have invested in heaven, were he to follow Jesus and let go of his affluence.

If we were to come face-to-face with Jesus today, have you, have I, identified the "one thing" that, like the wealthy young man, would evoke in us the response, "I'll do anything *but that* for you, Lord!" and send us away sad?

And in that one thing, can we perhaps recognize the one destiny for which we were created?

119

This One Thing?

The "one thing" each of us finds hardest to give up may be the single most significant sign to lead us to an entry door to our communion with God, if we could only recognize the importance of that choice. If we can identify the "idol" in our lives, we may also be able to put our finger on what God is asking of us, what he sees as a barrier between himself and us, and how, once that blockage is removed, he will satisfy those deeper desires of our hearts.

The human embryo, another kind of seed, grows to the point where it must risk entry into the world outside its mother's body. The human soul finds its truest destiny in God, and though each of us may seek satisfaction and significance in other things—service to our brothers and sisters, artistic endeavor, meaningful work, warm human relationships—it is only in God's presence, loving and pleasing him, that we will feel truly at home.

And knowing this, knowing us better than we know ourselves, knowing for what we have been created, God draws us—you and me—up to his light. Our progress isn't always easy. We encounter sticks or stones or mountain ranges in this quest. Our learning curve is steep. We keep slipping back, making side trips. But once we have heard the divine summons nothing else will seem adequate around which to structure our lives.

Wanting, But Not Yet Having

However, wanting God, and not being able to find him when we wish, or not having him to the degree of our desire, may leave us in a place of frustration, even despair.

A doctor friend of mine in Tanzania wrote one Easter:

As the Exodus was the central event in the Old Testament, so the Resurrection is in the New. As we look again at how biblical people experienced these events, we see hope, but not of the Hallmark greeting card variety. The Israelis crossed the Red Sea only to be faced with forty years of sand, thirst, boredom, no job satisfaction, and no control over that pesky cloud. The disciples faced the empty tomb, then had to wait forty days for Pentecost. Thomas was left hanging in doubt and disbelief for a whole week. Cleopas and his friend, on the way to Emmaus, were perplexed about the disappearance of Jesus, who had been their hope for the liberation of Israel. When he died, so did their hope. Then, when Jesus showed up and broke bread with them, "their eyes were opened and they recognized him, and he disappeared from their sight."

As soon as they understood, he was no longer with them! God's greatest acts sometimes leave us hanging. We, too, have those glimpses of knowing, of seeing something happen which confirms our faith. But since it is faith—which has to do with things not yet seen—we also live in the biblical experience of being left hanging.

Psychiatrist Gerald May says,

We have this idea that everyone should be . . . totally whole, totally together spiritually, and totally fulfilled. That is a myth. In reality, our lack of fulfillment is the most precious gift we have. It is the source of our passion, our creativity, our search for God. All the best of life comes out of *our human yearning—our not being satisfied.* Certainly Scripture and religious tradition point out that we are not to be satisfied. We are meant to go on . . . seeking. Paul tells the Greeks in Athens that God created us to seek him.

Oh, yes! I find myself saying: That's it exactly. It's the *longing* that draws us—like the longing of the growing seed-sprout for light, like an iron filing pulled by a magnet—towards the only One who can fulfill us. The thought of the Promised Land kept those angry, frustrated Hebrew people going for forty years in the wilderness. If everything were satisfaction and contentment and answered prayer and fig trees and vineyards and milk and honey, what would have motivated them to keep going?

And I would go even further than Gerald May. In studying the Beatitude that talks about the blessing of being hungry and thirsty for righteousness, I have wondered if that hunger and thirst had something to do with the longing C. S. Lewis described as *sehnsucht*, the desire to experience some poignant, holy, invisible beauty that is indescribable except for the conviction that when we find it at last, the joy will make sense of all the heartache and unfulfilled desire of our present world. We are not told *when*, but we are promised that "those who hunger and thirst . . . will be filled."

My son John, during a time of stress and difficulty in his medical training, longing for God's call and promise to be fulfilled in his life, wrote a poem based on Romans 8:25 where Paul tells us, "If we hope for what we do not yet have, we wait for it patiently." John's final stanza still reaches out and moves me whenever I reread it, not just because he wrote it, but because I join in our universal human longing to be with God, to have all my unsatisfied longings fulfilled:

> *Unless I am mistaken*
> *All of us wait for this—*
> *To jettison the grasping hands,*

To lope through new-created lands
Where hope and have may kiss.

Perhaps the growing seed wonders if it will ever pierce through the skin of soil and sod and burst into the light. This is, for me, a parable of the life of faith. It is across the gulf between the *wanting* and the *having* that faith carries us. Our belief in a God who is good, who understands our yearnings, who teaches us much by making us wait, and who will ultimately reward our upward struggle, allows us to persevere, to persist. As the author of *The Cloud of Unknowing* challenges us: "Smite upon the thick cloud of unknowing with the sharp dart of longing love; come what may, never give up."

I am reminded of the image of the moth and the candle in Annie Dillard's *Holy the Firm*, in which the moth's passion for the light draws it *into* the light of the flame, and it eventually becomes a charred attachment to the wick, a part of the wick in its self-immolation. This is the image of the Christian drawn by the God-flame that burns up our mortal elements and turns us into wicks to light the rooms of the world.

The Risk of Change

Once it has germinated, the seed cannot remain comfortable and quiescent in the heart of the earth. It must risk the upward thrust into a new element, a new dimension, where it will be exposed to wind, rain, drought, burning heat, and frigid cold. It is in this new area of risk that its only opportunity to bear flowers and fruit will be granted.

Growth. By its very definition, it is never static. All growth implies, and requires, change. And change suggests risk—a move into unknown territory, a step into the dark. This sounds dangerous, and it may certainly bring its perils with it, but it is also inevitable. Even those contented souls who find themselves at home with themselves in midlife and happy with their spouses, their circumstances, their accomplishments, must face, along with the maturing of wisdom, the slow aging of the body and the constraints that accompany that shift. I am very aware that though my energy level and my motivation remain high, I am limited in my physical activities. I can't climb mountain peaks like my sons. I need a nap in the afternoon. The names of familiar, well-loved people escape me from time to time. I find myself unintentionally double-booking appointments, and I often search for a word that floats just above my rim of recollection.

But I don't ever want to stop growing. And even death, inevitable as it is, will be just one more growth spurt into the future, one more growing edge, one more leap into the light. Remember, we don't die into death. We die into life! As Floyd Lotito says in *Wisdom, Age, and Grace*: "Death is not extinguishing the light; it is putting out the lamp, because the dawn has come."

The Growth Impulse

I have heard successful corporate executives who boast that they have "pulled themselves up by their own bootstraps" or make the claim, "I'm a self-made woman." Is it possible for us to grow spiritually simply by our own human effort? The longing to be close to God, to know his presence, to follow him, like David to "have a heart after him," ultimately to be like him, is a yearning implanted by God. (Writing that, I realize I have used a gardener's term—*implanted*!) St. Augustine talked about a heart-restlessness "until we find our rest in Thee." That void, that emptiness, that sense of being cut off from the only One who can satisfy our soul desire, is the means God gives to turn us in his direction, to magnetize us upwards to him. Yes, he gives the desire, and he then implements in us the means to move toward what we are searching for. Paul admits: "I planted the seed, Apollos watered it, but God made it grow. So neither he who plants nor he who waters is anything, but only God, who makes things grow. . . . For . . . you are God's field" (1 Corinthians 3:6–9).

What a splendid image! Can you see it in your imagination? The myriad grass stalks, their edges thin as green hair, along with oxalis, chicory, clover, their seed heads nodding in the wind, contours penciled with sunlight. A million greens, impossible greens, each blade seeming to be etched in with its individual colored pencil stroke. Even the early morning smell of dew on grass is like an act of praise, a fragrant incense rising to God. Each of us is a blade of grass growing up to God, indistinguishable in the mass, but individually valued and cared for by a Creator whose capabilities are infinite.

My friend Timothy Botts, the calligrapher, illustrated a poem of mine with this theme—the praise that rises from the created meadow to its Creator. His exquisite penmanship turned the letters of the alphabet into waving, grasslike flourishes in different shades of green. The poem's concluding line includes us humans ("like grass, like the flowers of the field," in Isaiah's phraseology) in the green equation: "Lord, now make of *our* hearts a field to raise your praise." I can consciously bring the poem to life when I find myself in a green field, and, quite without pantheism, align myself with the rest of creation in praising God.

Signs of Growth

One of the more rigorous spiritual disciplines is that of self-examination. For many people this seems like a negative. What can be gained by the navel gazing of morbid introspection? What good will it do to rehearse and re-rehearse my own flaws and faults? For women, the term "self-examination" may have come to mean the regular, systematic search of their bodies for lumps of cancer in a lymph node or a breast. (A frequent reason for neglecting this inspection for disease is fear. What if I do find something suspicious or threatening? Better to let the malignancy lurk unseen and unrecognized for as long as it can so that my emotions are not ruffled by dread or anxiety. We all recognize the shortsightedness of such a strategy.)

But self-examination also has its positive aspects—the search, not for disease but for healthy growth—the kind we expect to notice in our musculature from weight-training, the kind we look for in our children as we stand them up against the kitchen doorframe, marking their height month by month in an ascending stair of pencil lines that tell us our young ones are progressing as we had hoped.

I have written more than one poem using grass as a personal self-metaphor. One of them includes the line: "I can feel myself growing an inch an hour in the dark." Isn't it amazing how fast a newly cut lawn will grow back to its former shaggy state in less than a week? Be on the alert for the kind of growth in your soul that pleases God—growth in grace, in wisdom, in love, whether it comes fast, like the front lawn, or with agonizing slowness, like the oak tree.

If the fruits we bear are of the Spirit, it is well to acknowledge them. If the gifts we exercise are Spirit given, false modesty about them insults the Giver. If I can look at my life with a kind of holy penetration and sense that God is telling me, "Well done!" I need to assent to his evaluation and praise him that he who has begun a good work in me is continuing it.

Change, and Contrast

One spring in Illinois, my journal recorded a sudden weather change:

> All the rain, sleet, melting ice, and warming southerly winds mean that there is too much water for the sodden ground to absorb—and there's no place for it to go. Every ditch and furrow and stream brims and glitters with water. As I travel the country roads I see the sky reflected in places I've never seen it before!
>
> Each night the temperature dips. Frost catches and controls the flooding until the next day. But during last night's darkness the level of the river dropped dramatically, leaving the saplings along its banks collared with lacy scallops of ice, with the black water churning away two feet below.

Contrasts—warm to cold, high to low, shadow to brightness, slick to rough; as mortals without each we lose the meaning of the other in this mortal life. Without struggle and storm, the smooth, sunlit days would dream along, serene and unremarkable, taken for granted. If, on a scale of one to ten, everything is a ten, then a ten has no meaning (except in heaven). It carries significance only if we contrast it with a one or a two. Without the dark, hopeless stretches in our emotional or spiritual seasons we might get bored with blessing; grace might seem stale.

Epiphany, the showing light, the revelation—perhaps its very transience is what lends it its appeal. If our days were routinely sun filled, peaceful, tranquil, calm, predictable, stress free—their very serenity would soon seem flat, humdrum, monotonous. God allows the deep darkness to be tempered by starlight, moonlight, a glow of approaching dawnlight. His summer warmth is such a relief from winter chill that we feel the difference with our skins and eyes, and appreciate both light and warmth. There is purpose in the divine distinction between night and day, summer and winter, heat and cold.

William Stringfellow's perception, that God makes himself known to us "here and there, now and then," strikes me forcibly as being exactly the way I experience God. It's not that he only *comes* to us "here and there, now and then," but that, distracted and preoccupied as we are, we *perceive* him only sporadically, in bursts of intensity like an electrical power surge, rather than constantly in a steady stream of light.

Have you ever bicycled along a country road overhung with foliage from thick woods on either side? As you rode, the sun pierced between the tree trunks, dappling you with sudden sunlight between stretches of deep shadow. This lack of continuity speaks both to our lack of focus on God, of staying in the path of his light, as well as God's habit of surprising us with a vision of himself when we least expect it.

❧

Journal entry:

Camping in the snow at Tuolumne Meadows. The air is chill in the shade, but this morning I've found a lozenge-shaped patch of sun to sit and write my journal in. The sun blesses me for about ten minutes, writing its signature on my head and shoulders before moving its benediction to a tussock of grass, abandoning me once more to shade. Only a nomad can be perpetually sunstruck. I do not expect God to follow me with his warmth, like a puppy on my leash. I must watch where he goes, and follow him *there*.

Change and renewal dance into our lives dynamically, intersecting the humdrum, with its flatness and decay. And so I praise my Creator for building into our universe the sudden shifts, the contrasts of seasons, the infinity of space, the magnitude of mountain ranges like the Rockies or the Himalayas, as well as the gentle swelling of a small bud on a branch or a fleck of light shining through a leaf.

The Leap into Light

Have we gotten ahead of ourselves with all this talk about trees and vegetables and gardens? Let's return to where we accompanied our green sprout in its urgent flight upwards from seedhood to new existence above ground.

And *flight* doesn't seem to be too exaggerated a word to use. I've seen crocuses in very early spring, just before Easter, when ragged snow still cloaked the earth, pushing so fast that their tight, purplish buds, inches up from the soil since the night before, still wore a cap of snow crystals. It was a startling metaphor for Easter resurrection, which we celebrated a week later.

Seed. Sprout. Fledgling leaves. What next? Yes, the crocus is an apt illustration; Stage Four asks our plant to burst into flower and fruit. Move on with me, as we look at how our growing souls can grow tall, and move beyond our basic green, bursting into color, fragrance, and sweetness.

8

GREEN TREES FOR GOD

They shall be oaks of righteousness, the planting of the Lord.

ISAIAH 61

*Every forest branch moves differently
in the breeze, but as they sway
they connect at the roots.*

RUMI, PERSIAN POET

When you think "garden," do you instinctively think trees? Most of us don't. The usual garden is conceived of as low-level flower beds, with a few bushes or small saplings. Because full-grown trees are expensive and difficult to transplant, most landscape designers don't include them in their plans for new gardens.

Yet the tree, which with its height and shade gives a garden another dimension, is a significant part of more established garden communities. The tree is an image often used in Scripture for maturity and longevity. In Proverbs, Wisdom is imaged as a tree. Paul, in his letter to Ephesus, is using tree imagery in his phrase, "rooted and grounded in love," to refer to the stability of mature Christians. And in Colossians 1 and 2 several tree images appear in Paul's description of how the Gospel becomes rooted and growing and fruitful. Think of Paul's prayer in Colossians 2:9 as a picture of a tree growing like those who have heard and believed God's truth: "Continue to live in him, rooted and built up in him, strengthened in the faith as you were taught, and overflowing with thankfulness." Such imagery helps us to think imaginatively about our inward growth in God. If God likens me to a tree, what does he expect? What characteristics of a grown tree remind us of holy people, "saints," in New Testament terminology?

Endurance to Maturity

One such characteristic is toughness, particularly if we are talking about trees such as walnuts or oaks. If your house has oak floors or furniture, you know something of the beauty and durability of this wood. A dense-grained hardwood, it glows with a patina that, unlike pine or fir or other "softwoods," increases with age. This kind of toughness is usually achieved only by slow, steady growth. Quick-growing trees like birches, cottonwood, alders, or poplars spring up and flourish, but have a far shorter life span. Mighty oaks and redwoods and sequoias take longer to achieve their full, magnificent height, and they have an almost legendary longevity. Olive trees, rather than towering up, thicken outward until they are almost as wide as they are tall. Today, the ancient olive trees in the Garden of Gethsemane, just across the Kidron Valley from the Old City of Jerusalem, were probably standing there when Jesus was betrayed by Judas. And some sequoias and oaks have similar century-spanning life; nature's historians, their growth-rings telling the story of their centuries.

Jesus quoted from Isaiah 61, a chapter that came to have great personal consequence for me in the lonely time following my first husband's death. The promises it contains seem so perfectly designed for a heavy heart. "The

Spirit of the Sovereign Lord is on me," (says Isaiah, says Jesus), "to preach good news . . . to bind up the broken-hearted . . . to comfort all who mourn, and provide for those who grieve . . . to bestow on them a crown of beauty instead of ashes, the oil of gladness instead of mourning, and a garment of praise instead of a spirit of despair. They will be called oaks of righteousness, a planting of the Lord for the display of his splendor."

What a splendid description of an oak tree, crowned with the beauty of its early spring leaves, cloaked with green praise instead of the despair of winter snow. I took it to heart. I do want to be "an oak of righteousness, planted by the Lord to display his glory." But only after many seasons of fall, and falling leaves, and winter, frigid and bleak, will I have grown tall enough to fill that job description. The glory and beauty don't come cheap. They must be earned with perseverance and patience, through the seasons of life. And the growth, often so slow it seems barely perceptible, adds ring to annual ring from the core of the trunk outward, and inch to inch as upward growth occurs, until that maturity is gained. The scriptural counterpart is: "Add to your faith goodness; and to goodness, knowledge; and to knowledge, self-control; and to self-control,"—see how incremental this growth is!—"perseverance; and to perseverance, godliness; and to godliness, brotherly[/sisterly] kindness; and to [such] kindness, love. For if you possess these qualities in increasing measure, they will keep you from being ineffective and unproductive in your knowledge of our Lord Jesus Christ" (2 Peter 1:5 NIV).

Once again, the persistence and perseverance of trees tells us something about our own lives. Redwood trees have an almost uncanny ability to survive the holocausts of forest fires, retaining vital green foliage in spite of having the hearts literally eaten out of them by the flames. Madrona trees, those cinnamon-red, thin-skinned trees that decorate the cliff rocks of the Pacific coast, are able to embrace with young, healthy tissue their dead or damaged branches, the new growth, smooth as a well-tanned human arm, contrasting with the striated, gray deadwood, not rejecting it, but filling in the gaps and breaks and making the old wood a part of the pattern of the whole. Here are lessons for us in the human community; the old and the young need and benefit each other; age has important lessons for youth, and youth can invigorate age with its enthusiasm.

An older tree, by its very size, has value for its shade from heat and for its bulk, which can break the force of wind. It is no longer a slender sapling; its branches have spread and its leaves have thickened. Often the mature tree's root system is as extensive as its branch system, and those hidden root anchors, sucking up moisture and nutrients from deep below the soil's surface, make possible the sustained life of the large tree body above ground.

I am particularly fond of the promises in Psalm 92:12–5 (NRSV), promises about "the righteous," which, though I often feel unqualified to claim, I take very personally: "The righteous flourish like the palm tree, and grow like a cedar in Lebanon. They are planted in the house of the Lord; they flourish in the courts of our God. In old age they still produce fruit; they are always green and full of sap." I'm a senior citizen and a grandmother several times over, and my friends sometimes hint that a little more dignity might be in order. But God tells me I can be fruity and sappy and green! And I've just learned that date palm trees produce sweeter fruit the older they get. If the trees of the field clap their hands, as Isaiah assures us, why shouldn't we?

Purifiers

Leafy trees make invaluable contributions to earth's air and atmosphere, absorbing carbon dioxide and many other toxic pollutants. Christians, according to Jesus' admonitions in the Sermon on the Mount, have a similar function in their calling to be salt and light with all their cleansing and seasoning qualities.

Reinforcements

Even after they have been cut down, stripped of branches, derooted, debarked, and milled for lumber, trees, as the secret skeletons of our houses, unseen but still strong, are as supportive and significant as bones are to the human body. Think of all the uses we have for wood. Metals and plastics all have their practical applications, but wood, with its organic warmth and beauty, supplies a direct link between our homes and God's natural creation. All the more reason for us to use wood wisely, not wastefully, conserving it as one of our most worthy natural resources, and supporting reforestation, so that the supply will be replenished.

Landmarks

Driving through the flat prairie scenery of Iowa one early spring, while the landscape was still stark and spare and dun-colored, and before the buds had turned to leaves, I noticed fields where farmers were at work with their plows and disking machines, throwing up wakes of shining turf behind them. Some of those fields had a single tree standing centered in a wide stretch of plowed soil.

When I got to my destination for the night, a farmer's home near Iowa City, I voiced my question: "Why do farmers sometimes leave one lone tree standing in the middle of a field?" I got an eminently practical answer: "So that when they're plowing, they have something to rest the eye on. It helps them keep the furrows straight."

Since then, whenever I drive a prairie highway, I look for the lone trees—the plowman's navigational buoys set in seas of soil. And I ask myself: Can I be for someone else an interruption in the horizon, a landmark, a directional focus, a simplicity on which they can rest the eye and know they're going straight?

Individuality in Community

Most of us aren't called to live alone, in that kind of solitary simplicity. Most of us are more like trees that have the potential of being part of a forest, a gathering of kindred spirits, like-minded and planted in common ground. There will be seedlings, saplings, and grown trees, living together and supporting each other. Yet within those woods, as in the human community, each tree has its own individuality and uniqueness. No two trees, no two people are alike.

Lately, when my husband and I have taken our tent and gone camping in one of the many forest preserves that grace our West Coast, we've noticed that the rangers haven't been clearing away the debris of fallen trees or rotting tree trunks. When we've asked about this we've been told that these dead, decaying derelicts are ideal homes for bird and insect populations, which find the rotting wood hospitable, easy to penetrate and nest in. Transporting this into the realm of the spirit suggests the ways that those of us with experience and wisdom to offer, though we are past our prime, may provide nourishment, community, and a "habitat" for the young and growing.

Companion Branches

The large eucalyptus tree behind a friend's house caught my attention during a visit last year, its leaves small and slender, like little green knives. I was struck by the curious way the branches intertwined. It looked as though years ago a young branch had jutted out towards the house, and to prevent it from being a threat to the building as it grew heavier, it was bent back and wedged behind an older, upright branch, which held it in place so that it could grow *upwards* instead of *sideways.*

This image gave me a sense of, not stern restriction or negative force, but the comfort and reinforcement of enfolding arms. And of course, I identify myself, independent spirit that I am, with the potentially wayward branch. By God's grace the insubordinate energy in me has been redirected so that my life force no longer takes it own destructive, individualistic direction, but in becoming part of a community of intertwining boughs its strength and usefulness is augmented. It finds fulfillment, as I do, in thrusting skyward, part of a company of branches welcomed into the light.

Message-Carriers

My friend Amy Harwell, who out of her personal experience with cancer wrote the book *When Your Friend Gets Cancer: How You Can Help,* tells us:

> Not only can I now cope with my broken parts, I can accept the line in the Lord's prayer, *Thy will be done.* I knew I had reached this acceptance of God's will one day as I was driving down a country road. A tree caught

my attention—a beautiful pine with lush, spreading branches. Or it would have been—but all the branches had been sheared away on one side to allow the phone wires to pass.

I am that tree. Because God had other plans for me, I was pared away here and there to let loving messages come through for others.

Amy has taken that metaphor for herself, and she lives it out. God's messages, about love, and hope, and healing, continually come through her shorn "branches." She has become a signpost to others of how God can translate disease and suffering into a message of expectancy.

Have you ever walked in the woods on a windless autumn day when, as if by inaudible command, a scatter of golden leaves let go above you and began to float down from their parent branches, whispering their obedience, their "Yes" to God as they land on the forest floor and gild it seamlessly with their "gold leaf"? The trees in the forest listen to their Creator. With every season he murmurs his old-new words; they hear him attentively and obey him instantly. But we humans are different. A separate created order, we think of ourselves as infinitely more complex and clever, and we have been given some risky gifts—self-consciousness, reflective intelligence, imagination, and a free will that makes wide-reaching choices and decisions. Yet in spite of these advantages we have been rendered tone-deaf—by sin, by the babble of exterior and interior sounds that distract us from hearing God's whispered secrets. Although we ought to be gratefully returning our gifts to God, we choose more often to serve our own petty purposes and ignore his voice.

Unlike the trees, people aren't firmly rooted in one place. Free to move, we are constantly pulled off course by the multitude of invitations to alternatives. The small, interior voice of God is drowned out in human hubbub. When I read Jesus' urgent plea for followers who have "ears to hear," I feel his longing for true listeners. He wants his words to be made flesh, incarnated and lived out in each of us.

My prayer: *Lord, even as we're thinking about this process and how it should happen, are we hearing your voice with our inner ears? Yes. And as we walk among the flame-colored leaves and realize suddenly why autumn is called fall (the leaves in the still air begin to float down as if by your secret command to them), we know you are telling us about our own need to listen and obey. Open our inner ears wide and fill them with your messages.*

Signposts

In the Sierra Nevada, exposed to all the extremes of wind and weather, on the high rock domes at ten thousand feet, live the bristlecone pines, some of the oldest and hardiest of our conifers. In that constant stream of fierce air currents, the trunks and branches of these bristlecone pines are often dwarfed and molded into unique shapes. Just looking at them, we can determine the direction of the prevailing winds. I wrote about one such matriarchal tree:

> *You bend to an eternal gale.*
> *You are a signal*
> *to weather, a signpost in time*
> *pointing the way*
> *the wind went.*

Once again, can I draw the human analogy? Even in age, am I so molded by the wind of the Spirit that the shape of my life—its attitudes, actions, insights—is "a signpost in time," a model for those younger in faith?

Greenness

Yes. I've long ago left my seedling stage behind. Now my image for myself is that of a tree. Because my favorite color has always been green (my license plate in California reads FOLIO, a word that means both *leaf* and *page* and suggests my two passions, literature and nature) and I had titled my first two books of poetry *Listen to the Green* and *The Secret Trees*, back in the seventies I searched Scripture for images of verdure and vegetation to validate my own delight in greenery.

My first discoveries were disturbing. Throughout the prophecy of Isaiah, for instance, God levels his accusations of perversity at the people of Judah, charges that run like this: "Are you not a brood of rebels, the offspring of liars? You burn with lust among the oaks and under every green tree." Again and again, green trees on hilltops are described in Scripture as prime sites for the pagan orgies and fertility rites of idol worship and the people are told, in Deuteronomy 12:2, to "Destroy completely all the places . . . under every green tree where the nations . . . worship their gods." I was rather horrified at my finding. Did that mean that with my verdant images I was moving in the wrong direction, being false to God, and denying something central to godly belief? Then I recalled that trees, as created by God and growing in Eden, were part of the "very good" creation, and I found Hosea 14:8, a jewel of a promise in which the Lord God describes *himself* as "an evergreen tree" or "a green pine tree" (I later wrote a Christmas poem about "Jesus Evergreen"), and goes on to tell us to shun idols, for "your fruitfulness comes from me." This seemed to me like God's redemptive reversal of pagan worship, as if the Lord were saying: "You went off track into a worship of false gods, which involved rites that debased your humanity, and do not honor me, your true God. But now I'm showing you the reason why I created green and growth, why I delight in them, and what they *really* mean—health and life and holiness and the meaning of true worship. Look to me for life, not to trees or the wooden deities carved from them that can offer you nothing."

No. God isn't against green, but where his natural creation is perverted into falsehood and perversity, he asks us to replace the pagan images with his true ones. And the psalmists and prophets give us plenty of evidence that it is godly to be green.

Then again, the godly individual is likened, in Psalm 1:3, and Jeremiah 17:8 to "a tree that sends out its roots by the stream. It does not fear when heat comes; its leaves are always green. It has no worries in a year of drought and never fails to bear fruit."

During Advent and Christmas, millions of people spend millions of dollars purchasing Christmas trees that have been chopped from their roots in the evergreen forests, cocooned in chicken wire, and trucked across country, from Washington or Oregon or Wisconsin or Minnesota, to states where conifers such as blue spruce and Noble firs don't grow so easily or plentifully. Sure, they get beautifully decorated with tinsel and shiny ornaments, hung with fake fruit, flocked with artificial snow, often topped with an angel or a manmade star, electrified with colored lights, their raw stumps hidden under elaborate Christmas-tree skirts, and under their boughs Christmas gifts accumulate. But a month later, tinder dry and shedding their dead, faded needles, the same trees, no longer decked out for the holidays, are dumped on the street for pick-up and disposal by the "sanitary engineers."

I can't help making a comparison. If I were to choose between being an elaborately adorned Christmas tree and an unknown, unseen tree able to live out its life in a remote forest, living in clean light and strong air, with real stars nesting in its branches night by night, and real snow festooning it with white in winter, I wouldn't hesitate. The living tree would win out every time. Greenness means life.

A friend once told me, in winter, "Spring has three stages: the spring of light, the spring of running water, the spring of green." And of course those three stages work together; each one prepares for and encourages the next.

Light is a word with double meaning. The first harbinger of spring, light literally *lightens* us, easing from us the weight of winter. Each noon the sun arcs higher, and the nights shrink at their ends as the days stretch out, taking over, gathering the minutes into hours at each end of the diurnal cycle. As light lengthens and strengthens, the spring season is freed to lift and lighten our spirits. Because we are thus newly "lit," it seems as if this hopeful "lightness" penetrates our bones and translates itself into a buoyancy that is physical, as if gravity has lost some of its power and we can *spring*—leaping about with enthusiasm and cheerful ease, like people on the moon. We feel as if we have spring in our step, in more than one sense.

The spring of *running water*—I have walked through that too, when my eyes and my heart have overflowed with tears that matched the weeping from the sky and the flooding streams. And that is a vital part of growing. Combined with the increasing warmth that accompanies light, the running water—ice and snow thawing, of rain falling, filling our gutters, gurgling in our drainpipes, filling our ditches and furrows—ushers in the third element of spring, the vernal equinox—the spring of *green*. It is then that the verdant words in the Song of Solomon 2:10–12 become experiential for us: "My lover spoke and said to me, 'Arise, my darling, my beautiful one, and come with me. See! The winter is past; the rains are over and gone. Flowers appear on the earth; the season of singing has come.'"

My prayer: *Lord of my life, saturate me with your rain, toughen me in the strong winds of your Spirit, flow me green in the floodlight of your sunshine. Let me be a shade for someone's fatigue, and shapely enough for an artist to want to paint me into her landscape. May your small birds want to nest in me. May I be a landmark, a signpost to those who are confused or who have lost their way. As a "planting of the Lord," may I always be an image of strength and health in your kingdom.*

9

FLOWERS AND FRUIT

When at the Eucharist we offer back to God the firstfruits of the earth, we offer them not in their original form but reshaped by the hand of man; we bring to the altar not sheaves of wheat but loaves of bread, not grapes, but wine.

BISHOP KALLISTOS WARE

The Branch of the Lord will be beautiful and glorious, and the fruit of the land will be the pride and glory of the survivors in Israel.

ISAIAH 4:2

Gratitude is one of the first flowers to spring forth when hope is rewarded and the desert blooms.

KATHLEEN NORRIS IN *DAKOTA*

[God] has shown kindness by giving you rain from heaven and crops in their seasons; he provides you with plenty of food and fills your hearts with joy.

ACTS 14:17 (NIV)

This morning, following a gentle, all-night rain, the sun came out, and I was pulled, as by a magnet, out into the garden to inspect its state of mind, and mine, before getting to work on that mechanistic but indispensable

143

tool, my personal computer. I find I need this balance—between what is earthy, primitive even, but natural and fresh, and the technological tools that (supposedly) make my life more efficient and save me time.

Inside again, I carry with me the wet fragrance of my pink and white jasmine, as well as colors and textures—two in particular, the midnight blue, almost black, of some border pansies with their golden eyes and velvet petals, and the coral pink and tangerine of my Iceland poppies, their petals still crinkled like crepe paper from being so tightly folded inside the hairy green sheaths of their bud stage. They are fragile looking and impermanent; a day or two later, their petals have fallen like large confetti on the soil, where the pansies are hardy enough to withstand light frost.

But their beauty will carry me through the day.

What primary appeal do flowers have for us? Isn't it their fragrance? And their beauty? Imagine a wedding, or even a funeral, without flowers. They are one of the most welcome and necessary accompaniments for banquets, private dinners, anniversaries. The slogan "Say it with flowers" implies that where words, spoken or written, are inadequate, a bouquet of red roses or a spring flower arrangement or even a blooming potted chrysanthemum will help us express to the best-loved and appreciated people in our lives something of what they mean to us.

Flowers are perhaps the purest and most dramatic expressions of beauty found in nature. Their infinite variety of shapes, sizes, colors gives us dramatic and sensual evidence of God's unending creativity and experimentation. A quotation from Ann Haymond Zwinger, in *The Mysterious Lands*, caught my eye and made me wonder. I don't think I agree with her that "flowering is, after all, not an aesthetic in contribution, but a survival mechanism." Bees, other insects, and birds are drawn to flowers for their sweet nectar and fragrance, and in the process they assist the process of pollination, which assures the continued proliferation of a species. Even if flowers survive because of such attraction, beauty is a part of that attraction.

"We ... use the fruit of our gardens to prepare the bread of the sacrament," writes Vigen Guroian. Remember, though, the fruit of the garden is not restricted to what we eat. Every garden lends something extra to the imagination—beauty. The beauty of an artichoke or a potato may be more homely than the beauty of a daffodil in spring. But every garden holds the potential of giving us a taste of paradise. Sometimes this glory comes effortlessly, almost gratuitously (which is how grace works); sometimes only with prolonged effort and sweaty brows, someone laboring to make the garden grow—ecstasy as a result of agony.

It doesn't matter. Beauty comes essentially from God, for whom beauty is a virtue, and not just in the eye of the beholder. The Benedictines say that beauty is "truth shining into being," a principle adapted by John Keats with his famous line, "Beauty is truth, truth beauty." Is beauty merely a matter of personal taste? To a degree, yes. Otherwise we wouldn't have such an extraordinary diversity of clothing styles, decorating styles, architectures, art and music and dance forms, across the centuries and the continents. There appears to be a universal human impulse that moves beyond pragmatism towards beauty, which is further refined into art.

Art is what we say, what we sing, what we show (either in body movement or in the creative work of our hands) about what is welling up within us, bubbling like a pot on the boil. It cries out, as do the beauties of the natural world, for recognition and response. We want to share the creative part of ourselves, and so we have poetry readings and art exhibits and concerts and square dances and fashion shows and coffee table books and quilting bees.

If we're honest, we will all admit that we have been moved by such aesthetic impulses. Who among us has not doodled, written a love poem, decorated an Easter egg or a Christmas tree or our living room, or dug a bed for flowers? And when we got dressed this very morning, were we interested simply in being warm and comfortable and practical and decent? Didn't we care, just a bit, about how we appear to other people?

And beauty is important to God. He loves it. He made it. Why else would he shape and color fish, birds, insects, plants, and people with such astonishing diversity? As my friend Elizabeth Rooney once said, "Imagine making something as useful as a tree, as efficient at converting sunlight into food and fuel, as huge and tough as a white oak that can live three hundred years, and then decorating it in spring with tiny, pink leaves and pale, green tassels of blossoms?"

A God of Beauty

And beauty is an integral part of the nature of God. Although I haven't seen any statement to that effect from the systematic theologians, it seems clear to me in such Pentateuchal passages as those that describe the design of the biblical Tabernacle and the Temple, that design and beauty are important to God. The phrase "for glory and for beauty," rather mundanely translated "dignity and honor" in the NIV, exalts the sensuous and worshipful aspects of the clothing planned for the Levitical priests, as well as the implements and furnishings of the Holy Place, and the Holy of Holies—the space carved out for God in the Tabernacle. The high priest's robe, described in Exodus 28:33, was to be fashioned with "pomegranates of blue, purple and scarlet yarn around the hem . . . with gold bells between them." Here we find pattern, color, and sound all working together.

"For glory and for beauty." In other words, glory to reflect the splendor of Jehovah and beauty because the Lord delighted in it and wanted his people to enjoy it too. As Gene Edward Veith has said in *The Gift of Art:* "Beauty is an appropriate end in itself—the garments were made for beauty. The inventor of color, of form, of texture, . . . values the aesthetic dimension for its own sake. According to the clear statements of Scripture, art has its place in the will of God."

Phrases such as "the beauty of holiness" (2 Chronicles 20:21; Psalms 29:2; 96:9), "the beauty of the Lord" (Psalm 27:4), "Out of Zion, the perfection of beauty, God shines forth" (Psalm 50:2), "Let the beauty of our Lord be upon us" (Psalm 90:17), "Strength and beauty are in his sanctuary" (Psalm 96:6), "Your eyes will see the king in his beauty" (Isaiah 33:17), ". . . to give [them that mourn in Zion] beauty instead of ashes" (Isaiah 61:3).

Jesus talked fondly of the beautiful "lilies of the field" and of the Father's care for them in their dependency and fragility. For all its appeal, beauty's frailty and its temporal nature are emphasized. The phrase "beauty [is] a fading flower" appears repeatedly. There are warnings to all of us to avoid the temptation to prideful beauty. Superficial beauty, of face, of hair, of jewels, of clothing, is disdained in

Scripture in favor of beauty of character, or inherent, essential beauty, which springs from within. But none of these exceptions cancels out the fact that the Creator is responsible for the beauties we all acknowledge and enjoy, with what C. S. Lewis in his poem "A Confession" calls our "stock responses"—our innocent delight in the glory of "peacocks . . . silver weirs, new-cut grass, wave on the beach, hard gem, the shapes of horse and woman, Athens, Troy, Jerusalem."

I once read the 1870 journal of a prairie woman who noted about the quilts she made by hand, "I make them warm to keep my family from freezing. I make them beautiful to keep my heart from breaking." It doesn't take too much imagination to fill in the blanks of her story. Isolated during the winter months in a sod house in the vastness of the snow-sheathed prairie, her hunter husband gone for days at a time, checking his traplines, her children shut in with her to survive the frigid winters, without much nourishment for body or for soul, she turned to her own ingenuity to remedy the lack. In her quilts, their "raw-cut, uncolored edges" mirroring her own spare way of living, their colored pieces cut from scraps of calico, from worn-out clothes, she was able to create new and enchanting patterns. Under her fingers, painfully, stitch by small stitch, were formed the wedding ring and double star patterns. Her frozen soul was thawed with the beauty she herself had made from cast-offs. As Frederick Buechner has said in *Whistling in the Dark*: "Beauty is to the spirit what food is to the flesh. It fills an emptiness in you that nothing else under the sun can."

Yes, beauty is of God, the author of design and pattern and form, and we are made in his image, to respond to such loveliness with gratitude. Is it any wonder we love flowers?

And Fruit

All year long, in our small northern California town, and up and down the towns and cities of the West Coast, farmers from the central valleys hold their weekly produce markets. Ours falls on a Sunday, and early in the day, before the parking plaza behind our main street has had a chance to fill up with cars, the stalls and booths are set up to display the gorgeous fresh fruits and vegetables from the San Joaquin Valley. By noon, after church has let out, we join the throng of Sunday after-churchers moving from stall to stall to buy produce freshly picked that very morning and driven here for our convenience and delight. The colorful displays all offer samples—apple and orange and nectarine slices, creamed honey dipped up on wooden sticks, chunks of silky avocados. Almonds and pecans and walnuts gleam at us next to dried apricots and figs, huge green artichokes, cucumbers like submarines, purple eggplants, mushrooms in a dozen different shapes and shades, exotic salad mixes garnished with red and orange nasturtium blooms (this *is* California!), dried flowers and fresh flowers in pots, and the lushest red tomatoes imaginable.

I have a fellow feeling with these farmers. Not that my own farming has ever involved more than a backyard plot with a few rows of corn, beans, tomatoes, and lettuce. But I know the savory satisfaction of picking tomatoes, pickling gherkins, canning green beans, harvesting corn that I have grown myself from seed. Nothing is sweeter. Nothing makes better relish than home-grown corn, canned in pickle jars, row on golden row waiting in the closet to color the bleak winter with its crunch and tang.

Fruit is a central scriptural metaphor. Paul is quite blatant about it, though botanically not quite correct (but no matter) when he describes the fruit of the Spirit and talks of nine different varieties on a single tree! We can go down the list, along the tree branch, checking off those that we feel happy about—whose juice and sweetness, maturity and tang are enjoyed by the other people in our lives as well as those that have not yet come to perfect ripeness in us (ripeness to perfection takes time):

- Love (which is the only thing to heal a broken world)
- Joy (the exuberance that overflows our lives when we are at peace with God)
- Peace (the tranquillity that comes from confidence in our Father)
- Patience (which makes us willing to play the waiting game, and give ourselves time to grow)
- Kindness (the outworking of love)
- Goodness (the holiness that is beautifully and unselfconsciously at work in us)
- Faithfulness (loyal commitment)
- Gentleness (achieving God's goals by love, not force)
- Self-control (the ability to direct our energies wisely)

Paul gives us a shorter list in Ephesians 5:9: "Live as children of light (for the fruit of the light consists in all goodness, righteousness and truth)."

It was fruit with which the serpent tempted Eve in the first garden. Isn't it good of God—a part of his redemptive grace—to give us instead life-fruit that signifies not our departure from God in rebellion but our new growth, our renewal, in him? The Spirit sap and oil rises in our veins. His sun and warmth and nourishment produces leaves, flowers and, at last, the fruit, which is the end product of growth. It's like dessert at the end of a meal—sweet and delicious.

Incarnational Fruit

Whether or not we ever bear fruit in our own bodies through the physical birth of our children, we may all be true fruit bearers. The Incarnation (Enfleshment) enacted by God in Mary's body was not only a real, historical event but also a resplendent picture of the way the Holy Spirit may impregnate each one of us. It makes no difference if we are young and fertile (as Mary was) or well on in years (like Abraham and Sarah, or Zechariah and Elizabeth). Our nationality or social status is irrelevant. It doesn't matter if we are male or female, the phrase "Christ in you, the hope of glory" gives us infinite confidence that Christ may be conceived in us. In whom were, and are, the fruit-of-the-Spirit qualities most clearly and potently seen? In Jesus. Jesus himself is the fruit that God, through the Spirit, purposes to bear in us, growing in us "as a tender plant," living out his life through our lives, indwelling us, changing us from the inside out.

It is God's desire to indwell us, to plant himself at the core of our being, to impregnate us with Jesus-life, to rescue us from emptiness, aloneness, independence, barrenness, to grow Christ in us, and through him, the nine fruits of the Spirit.

Years ago, I wrote a poem about Mary and the visitation of God into her being. It began,

An apple is meant to be
flower & food & tree
& if it goes to rot
what of its destiny?

The poem was really attempting to probe the physical and spiritual needs of a woman "planned to be manned," yet still single, never experiencing the joyful fruit of children in her life, and to imagine God's strong, tender response to her need for fulfillment and fruitfulness. The poem, which emphasized the personal, intimate relationship between God and a human being, ended with these words:

His purpose finds
her heart of hearts,
conceiving Jesus
at her core
by his most
Holy Ghost. Once more,
as with lonely Mary, he
makes of her
in her own time
& in his time
his sweet bride, also a tree
thick enough to climb,
with petals
for the eye's delight,
& fruit to eat.

Some of those who read the poem (I sent it out as a Christmas card) were offended by the idea of representing God's entry into us in such jarring sexual terms, forgetting that the symbolism of countless biblical passages is frankly sexual, referring to the primal patterns of initiation and response between male and female. The history of God's ongoing involvement with his people is repeatedly expressed in the arresting imagery of the divine Lover desiring the devotion and loyalty of virgin Israel.

In the Old Testament, Jehovah was in love with Israel, calling her to be his consort. After the resurrection of Jesus, his covenant love is extended to include the church, that mysterious unity of all Christian believers, Jew or Gentile. God's passionate love still pursues a bride. In all four gospels Jesus is pictured as Bridegroom. In Ephesians 5 the human, husband-wife relationship is compared to the heavenly Christ-bride union.

What If It Goes to Rot?

In fall California farmers celebrate with pumpkin festivals; the fields and foothills blaze orange with pumpkins, and the closer you approach them the larger they loom, plump and rounded and colorful as fall foliage. Halloween is approaching, and on the weekends thousands of vans and station wagons loaded with young families make their pilgrimage to the pumpkin fields. There's an annual contest for the Largest Pumpkin, and monsters of hundreds of pounds of misshapen squash flesh are weighed and celebrated. After Halloween the same fields are still spotted with this fruit of the vine, but now only the rejects are left—the ones no one chose, that were flat on one side or scarred or just plain too ugly even for a jack-o'-lantern. All that growth, all summer long, for nothing? All that plump, sturdy pumpkin flesh simply waiting to go to rot?

In the hot noon sun of a summer day, I once went with two of my daughters, Robin and Kristin, and my granddaughter Lindsay, to a "u-pick" raspberry farm, where acres of bushes grow in green rows, from which you can pick your own berries and save some pennies. There we plucked, for eating and for making jam, twelve pounds of raspberries—huge hybrids, sweet, red-velvet pendants ripe enough to drop into our hands and thence into the plastic buckets slung around our necks.

As we slowly passed between the tall green thickets of bushes, starting and stopping, our fingers stained, our mouths tart with the taste of summer, we would be sure we had thoroughly stripped a certain bush. Then, as we crouched lower, we could see from a new angle all the hidden treasures that remained—berries hanging like red hearts, hiding behind the leaves, waiting for our nimble fingers.

I felt sad for the ones that never got picked (no one took the trouble to go slowly enough or search for them carefully enough), for the ones that seemed too small or too hard to reach. All that slow ripening, as the rains fell and the short, cool days turned long and warm—for nothing—fruit without fruitfulness.

Unpicked raspberries are like the ideas we never discover because we are too hurried, because we see or think superficially. Discarded pumpkins are like the precious people we ignore. They are like the images of the holy hinted at in creation. They are like the glimpses of God we miss because our eyes are half-closed or our attention distracted. Harvesting ideas, loving ordinary people, seeing correspondences between the seen and unseen worlds, and gleaning glimpses of God—such tasks, the same as berry picking, take time, thoroughness, concentration, and the willingness to crouch in the sandy soil, to peer upwards, to lift aside the raspberry leaves, to see deep into the heart of each bush, to penetrate its leafy green reality and value what we find there.

How odd that God humbles himself to be seen in the most ordinary beauties, the everyday, taken-for-granted stuff of creation! Yet his image is stamped wherever we turn our eyes. The clues to divine reality are under our feet, they brush our hands, they rustle in our ears, they mark our bare legs with their sharpness, and they burn our retinas with their color.

Thomas à Kempis, in *The Imitation of Christ*, reassures us, "If your heart is straight with God, then every creature will be to you a mirror of life and a book of holy doctrine." We are faced so often with things we know but still need to learn. How marvelous it is that realities as mundane as sunlight, field lilies, apple trees, ripe berries, pumpkins, and the delighted cries of young children are lenses through which we may see God.

> *"Lord, open thou our eyes, that we may behold wondrous things out of your word, out of your world. Seed us with the life of Jesus. Grow in us the fruit of the Spirit. May we be beautiful with your holiness. Amen."*

EPILOGUE

The garden has given us the pattern—production and reproduction rather than consumption. Origination. Procreation.

Before I found John, and not long after I lost Harold and had begun the long and tedious business of learning to live alone, piecing my life together again, my friend Carolyn left a magnetic motto on my refrigerator door. It read, "LIVE GENERATIVELY!"

We talked about it. Age has little to do with it. We were both sixtyish, but both had seventy- and eighty-year-old friends who lived as vitally as twenty-year-olds, friends like Madeleine L'Engle, whose purpose is to be "a universe-disturber for good."

It was a salutary reminder to me not to recede into the numbness and paralysis of bereavement, not to live at the mercy of events, but to continue to live a life that contributes to the energy of the world, that gives back as much as it takes. I needed to allow God's green and growth back into my life instead of subsiding onto an ash heap, Job-like. I asked God, believing, to clothe me with "a garment of praise instead of a spirit of despair."

Soul growth begins when we actively embrace ourselves, even in seeming failure. It took a while, just as a new plant takes a while to become itself, but living generatively, cultivating my soul soil, learning to live again as a single, and then a married woman again—decisive, exploratory, creative, honest, unafraid—became the call of God to me. He was the Gardener of my soul, who restored the springtime green that mourning had eroded away.

Who took the initiative in this generative process, God or me? It seemed like a series of small steps: God shows me a gift of green promise. I turn my head to look. He holds it out to me. I move closer, still a bit tentative. God says, "Here, take it, it's for you!" I respond, "Really? Are you sure?" He puts it in my hands. *"Yes!"* My fingers close over it, pull it close, affirm it. Hug it. Thank him. His eyes are warm with love.

This is the promise that became my experience. Though my life has not been one of uninterrupted sunshine, though I have sometimes allowed weeds to grow or been attacked by drought or disease, I can affirm the truth of God's assurance: "You will go out in joy and be led forth in peace; the mountains and hills will burst into song before you, and all the trees of the field will clap their hands. Instead of the thornbush will grow the pine tree, and instead of briers the myrtle will grow. This will be for the Lord's renown" (Isaiah 55:12–13).

> *For as the soil makes the sprout come up*
>   *and a garden causes seeds to grow,*
> *so the Sovereign Lord will make righteousness and*
> *praise spring up.*

ISAIAH 61:11

Printed in the United States
107429LV00001B/154-162/A

9 781573 832427